How to
Make Money
from Property

If you want to know how . . .

Buying a House
A step-by-step guide to buying your ideal home

Buy to Let Property Hotspots
Where to buy property and how to let it for profit

Buy to Let in France
How to invest in French property for pleasure and profit

Property Hotspots in London
Where in our capital city to buy and let property for profit

The Buy to Let Handbook
*How to invest for profit in residential property and
manage the letting yourself*

For more information on property:
Subscribe to www.propertyhotspots.net for up to the
minute information on property prices, property search,
estate agents, letting agents, property auctions,
100% mortgage providers, buy to let mortgage
providers and much more.

howtobooks

Send for a free copy of the latest catalogue:

How To Books
3 Newtec Place, Magdalen Road,
Oxford OX4 1RE, United Kingdom
E-mail: info@howtobooks.co.uk
www.howtobooks.co.uk

How to Make Money from Property

The expert guide to property investment

ADAM WALKER

howtobooks

Published by How To Books Ltd,
3 Newtec Place, Magdalen Road,
Oxford OX4 1RE, United Kingdom.
Tel: (01865) 793806. Fax: (01865) 248780.
email: info@howtobooks.co.uk
http://www.howtobooks.co.uk

First edition 2000
Reprinted 2002 (twice)
Reprinted 2003 (three times)

British Library Cataloguing in Publication Data.
A catalogue record for this book is available from
the British Library.

Edited by Francesca Mitchell
Cover design by Baseline Arts Ltd, Oxford

Produced for How To Books by Deer Park Productions
Typeset by Kestrel Data, Exeter
Printed and bound by Cromwell Press Ltd, Trowbridge, Wiltshire

NOTE: The material contained in this book is set out in good
faith for general guidance and no liability can be accepted
for loss or expense incurred as a result of relying in particular
circumstances on statements made in the book. Laws and
regulations are complex and liable to change, and readers should
check the current position with the relevant authorities before
making personal arrangements.

Contents

Part 2 – Buying a Property to Let

Preface

'Many of the world's richest people have made their fortunes from property.'

Now you can make money from property too – if you are careful. This book will show you how to spot property investment opportunities and how to avoid all the most common mistakes. In particular it will show you:

- How to buy a house that is likely to appreciate in value.

- How to refurbish a property to sell.

- How to deal with builders, architects, surveyors, estate agents and planning consultants.

- How to buy a property to let.

- How to raise the finance.

- How to calculate the likely returns.

- How to become a full-blown property developer.

Whether your objective is to add a little to your income in retirement or to become a full-time property developer, this book will show you how to make money from property.

Professionals such as estate agents are referred to in general terms as 'he'. This is to make the book easy to read and should be considered an inclusive term that does not imply that all such professionals are male.

Adam Walker

NOTE

Prices given in the case studies are illustrative and are not intended to reflect the actual value of properties in the stated areas.

Thank you for buying one of our books. We hope you'll enjoy the book, and that it will help you make money from property.

We always try to ensure our books are up to date, but contact details seem to change so quickly that it can be very hard to keep up with them. If you do have any problems contacting any of the organisations listed at the back of the book please get in touch, and either we or the author will do what we can to help. And if you do find correct contact details that differ from those in the book, please let us know so that we can put it right when we reprint.

Please do also give us your feedback so we can go on making books that you want to read. If there's anything you particularly liked about this book – or you have suggestions about how it could be improved in the future – email us on info@howtobooks.co.uk

Good luck with making your fortune!

The Publishers
www.howtobooks.co.uk

Part One

MAKING MONEY FROM YOUR OWN HOME

Introduction

These days, home buyers are bombarded with advice on mortgages, life insurance and endowment policies but very few people receive any advice on what sort of property to buy. I find this rather strange. The wrong choice of mortgage could certainly cost many thousands of pounds over its full term but the wrong choice of property could be financially catastrophic. Consider this true example.

John Smith bought a two-bedroom flat in Redland, an up-market suburb of Bristol, for £8,500 in 1979. He sold it in 1997 for £79,950 – an increase of 941%.

Steven Brown also bought a house in 1979. He paid £18,000 for a three-bedroom ex local authority house in Southmead, a less desirable area of Bristol just a few miles away. In 1997 he sold this property for just £18,500 – an increase of only 3% in 15 years!

This story is dramatic evidence of just how volatile and patchy the housing market can be. Such volatility creates winners and losers. This section will help you to be a winner in the property appreciation game.

1

Thinking it Over

YOUR HOME AS AN INVESTMENT

By far the easiest way to make money from property is through investing wisely in your own home. There are three reasons for this.

1. It is much easier to raise money to buy a home than it is to raise money for property development.

2. The interest costs are much reduced. If property is left empty whilst it is being refurbished you will need to deduct the cost of interest before calculating your profit. If you are able to live in a property whilst you are refurbishing it, you can offset the mortgage or rental payments that you would have made anyway against the interest costs.

3. Most importantly of all, the profit that you make from selling your own home is usually tax free.

These three factors together make your home a wonderful and very easily realisable investment opportunity. I have therefore devoted the first section of this book to considering the various ways in which you can maximise the investment potential of your own home.

ASSESSING THE COST

Nothing in life is free and the cost of treating your own home as an investment opportunity should not be underestimated. The main drawbacks are as follows.

Noise, dust and mess
Living on a building site is not a lot of fun. If you or your family can't face the thought of your possessions being covered in

dust or spending a whole winter without heating then property development might not be for you.

Inappropriate accommodation

The property that represents the best investment opportunity will often not be the property that is most appropriate to your family's accommodation needs. You will need to be prepared to make compromises here in order to maximise your returns.

Social consequences

Most properties can be refurbished within a year. Moving house every 12 months can be very destructive, particularly if you have school-age children.

Financial risk

All investments have a degree of risk and investing in property is no exception. Hundreds of thousands of people lost money in the last property crash in 1988 and it could easily happen again.

Despite the risks, property investment can produce some excellent returns. The following case studies are intended to help you to decide on the risk and reward ratio that is right for you and your family.

CASE STUDIES

Case study 1

Sarah G brought her first property right at the bottom of the last recession in the property market in January 1992. She chose a two-bedroom flat in Acton, London W3. She would have preferred to buy in Ealing or Chiswick but both areas were out of her price range and she thought Acton, being so close, might be an up-and-coming area.

The flat was in a terrible condition. It had been occupied for many years by an elderly lady. It had no heating, an ancient kitchen and bathroom and had not been redecorated for many years. Sarah paid £24,000 for it.

Over the next six months Sarah camped in the sitting room whilst the flat was refurbished. For the first three months she had no kitchen or bathroom so she lived on take-away food and sandwiches and showered at work. Sarah found an excellent builder to do most of the work but to save money she did the decoration herself, often working until 11 o'clock at night.

Sarah's hard work paid off when she sold the refurbished flat for £52,000 in September 1992. Building works had cost her £9,000 and estate agency and other fees came to another £2,000 leaving her with a net profit of £16,000.

Sarah's next purchase, made in September 1992, was a three-bedroomed terraced house around the corner. The elderly owner had recently died and Sarah bought it privately from her son for £55,000 – an excellent price.

This property too was in very poor condition and Sarah suffered considerable personal inconvenience whilst it was refurbished. In September 1993 she sold the finished house for £92,000. The cost of refurbishment was £12,000 and other fees came to £4,000, giving Sarah a net profit of £21,000.

Unfortunately, Sarah's third attempted purchase fell through on survey due to subsidence problems and she had to sleep on a friend's sofa for three months. However, in January 1994 she managed to buy a four-bedroom Edwardian semi-detached house also in Acton for £105,000. This property was also in poor condition but Sarah was attracted by its wonderful period features. Sarah spent £19,000 on building works which included replacing the kitchen and bathroom, rewiring, replumbing, redecorating and landscaping the overgrown garden. In April 1995 she sold the property for £175,000, giving a net profit of £46,000.

Sarah immediately bought a five-bedroom detached house in Ealing Common for £205,000. This property was in much better condition than the others but it was decorated throughout in 1970s orange and brown. This enabled Sarah to buy it quite cheaply. In September 1996 she sold it for £285,000, giving her a net profit of £50,000.

Sarah's final purchase in September 1996, was a six-bedroom detached house in Ealing, London W5 – the area that she had originally wanted to live in. The house had been repossessed by a building society and had been empty for over a year. It was in a shocking state. It had been badly vandalised and many of the fixtures and fittings had been stolen. Worst of all, Sarah's surveyor picked up a serious dry rot infestation in the cellar. Sarah bought the property for £150,000 and spent another £100,000 on the necessary building works. Nine months later she owned a fully refurbished house worth approximately £400,000. In the three years since then, property prices in West London have soared and by January 2000 Sarah owned a property worth more than three quarters of a million pounds.

Commenting on her experience Sarah said, 'I have made an excellent return from my development activities but I have really paid the price. For more than five years I have lived in squalor and worked 18 hours a day holding down a full-time job to pay the mortgage and working as a decorator during the evenings and weekends. This has left me no time for anything else at all. Nevertheless, today I own a £750,000 house with a very small mortgage so I feel that it was worth it. However, I am taking a break from property development for the time being so that I can spend a bit more time on my social life.

Case Study 2

Warren P bought a four-storey house in Harlesdon, London NW10 for £65,000 in July 1987 – the peak of the last boom in the property market. He planned to convert the property into four flats which would together be worth about £220,000. Warren intended to live in one of the flats and sell the others. He financed the purchase with £30,000 of his own money, a £60,000 mortgage and a £60,000 loan from his father.

Warren's development went wrong almost immediately. He had problems getting planning permission, which caused a four month delay. The building work cost far more than expected and following a row about costs, the builder walked off the job in June 1988. Then just as the flats were finally ready, the market collapsed. By the time the last flat was sold Warren had lost £60,000.

Commenting on his experience Warren said, 'I got my fingers very badly burned. Everyone else was making money from property and I thought I could too. I have lost all my savings, I have lost my home and I still owe my father £30,000. It has been a financial disaster. I wish I had stuck to what I know.'

Case Study 3

John and Catherine C bought a very dilapidated detached three-bedroom house with a three quarters of an acre plot in Gerrards Cross, Buckinghamshire for £200,000 in January 1995. John and Catherine have three children and they were really looking for a four-bedroom house in a cheaper location nearby. However, they both felt that the house in Gerrards Cross would be an excellent investment.

John and Catherine did not have the money to do all the building work in one go, so they did as much as they could themselves and had builders in as they could afford it to handle the more difficult jobs. As a result, the refurbishment took three years. They hated the mess and disruption and the two younger children hated having to share a bedroom. They also complained loudly that Mum and Dad never had time to play with them like other parents.

Nevertheless, John and Catherine were right about the property's investment potential. Between 1995 and 2000 property prices in Gerrards Cross went through the roof and today their almost fully refurbished property is worth nearly half a million pounds.

Commenting on their experience Catherine said 'I still don't know if buying this house was the right thing to do. It's turned out to be a wonderful investment but it has taken a lot of our time and it is still too small for us. However, the four-bedroom house down the road that we nearly bought is only worth about £350,000 so we have been well rewarded for our compromise.'

2

Choosing the Right Area

UNDERSTANDING THE IMPORTANCE OF AREA

The three most important factors in valuing a property are location, location and location. So goes the old estate agent adage and this one is 100% true.

A smaller property in a better area will nearly always be a better buy than a larger property in a poorer one. This is part of a long-term social trend. The gap between the rich and the poor is growing ever wider. A direct consequence of this is that the value of property in the better residential areas is appreciating more quickly than the value of property in the less desirable areas. There are three reasons why buyers who can afford it are prepared to pay a premium to live in the 'right' area.

Social benefits

Most people are happiest living in an area where there are other people like them. For example, people with a young family like to know that there are other young families in the area. They would find it hard to feel at home in an area where the majority of their neighbours are students.

Fear of crime

Crime, or more accurately the fear of crime, is another important factor that is encouraging people to head for the relative safety of the established residential areas.

Schooling

Until recently we were led to believe that all schools were the same. The publication of the school league tables has dispelled this myth forever and property within the catchment area of the better schools is increasing in value disproportionately.

If you are buying a property with its investment potential in mind, my advice would be to compromise on the property or its situation rather than the area.

SPOTTING THE UP-AND-COMING AREAS

Some of the most dramatic gains have been made by home owners who bought property in an up-and-coming area. Property values in some parts of London doubled during the three years from 1997 to 2000. If you are single or married without children, you might want to gamble on buying a property in an up-and-coming area. However, gamble is the right word to use here. The desirability of an area can change very quickly and even the professionals often get caught out. Consider the following examples.

Losing value

In one suburb of Manchester, property has halved in value during the last five years. The problem started when a housing association bought a few houses and moved some problem tenants in. The existing residents found their new neighbours difficult to live with and those that could sold their properties and left the area.

The sudden increase in the number of properties available led to a drop in prices and this in turn made the area more attractive to the housing association who bought up more properties. This changed the residential mix of the area permanently and the last of the original residents felt so uncomfortable that they also left. Today the area is almost entirely owned by housing associations and is controlled by problem tenants. It is now such an undesirable place to live that values have plummeted.

Increasing value

The opposite can also occur with equal speed. A good example of an area where prices have increased in the last five years would be West Acton in West London. West Acton is next to Ealing, which has always been a desirable area. Most of the houses are large Victorian and Edwardian properties with four or five bedrooms.

During the 1970s and 80s many of these houses were considered too large for single family occupation and were split up into flats and bedsits. Now the trend is being reversed. Prices in Ealing rose to such a level that many families could no longer afford to buy there. West Acton was a logical alternative. The properties were very similar to those in Ealing. Transport links were good and the area was within the catchment areas for some good schools.

The trickle of professional families moving into the area became a flood and prices increased sharply. The original residents, mostly young people living in small flats, no longer felt at home and began to move out to more cosmopolitan areas. Today West Acton is almost indistinguishable from Ealing.

ASSESSING AN AREA

If you don't know the area that you are intending to buy in, it is well worth spending some time getting to know it properly. First impressions can be very deceptive and ideally you should visit the area at least three times, once on a weekday, once at night and once at a weekend. It is surprising how many apparently quiet streets are plagued by problems such as commuter traffic during the rush hour or gangs of marauding teenagers after dark.

Here are some other useful ways to size up an area.

- Visit the local shops – do they sell the sort of things that you buy?

- Visit the local pubs – do you feel at home with the locals?

- Look at the gardens – are they well maintained and what play equipment is there? This will give you an idea of the ages of the local children.

- Count the number of bells on each door – more than one means that the house has been split into flats. This could mean noise and parking problems.

- Look (discretely) through the windows – the curtains, decor and furnishings will give you a good idea of the age and background of the people who live there.

- Check out the local transport – try actually doing the journey to work before you commit yourself.

- Check out the schools – the league tables are not perfect but they give a good idea of the quality of schooling in the area.

CHOOSING THE SITUATION

Location is not the same as situation. By comprising over the situation, you might well be able to avoid making compromises in other areas. For example, a house on a busy road might sell for 20 or 30% less than an identical house round the corner. Places to look for bargains include:

- On a busy road
- near a railway line
- under a flight path
- out of easy reach of shops
- outside the catchment area of good schools
- next to an industrial or business site
- above a shop.

Look for one special feature

A tip that had served me well is to try to buy a property with at least one special feature. For example, an unusual window or fireplace, an aga or one unusually large room. A house in a road of a hundred identical properties will never really excite a buyer because they know that if they lose this one there will always be another. A more unique property generates much more excitement because buyers know that if they miss it they will never find one like it.

The 'uniqueness factor' can drive up the sale price and your investment return considerably. One of my clients told me a particularly dramatic story to support this point. It concerned an exceptionally pretty thatched cottage in Banbury which was worth about £300,000 but sold for £450,000 because two competing buyers were quite determined to have it.

If you are buying a property with an eye to its future value, my advice would be to try to buy one of the smaller and cheaper houses in the road or, if you can afford it, a unique property in a rural or semi-rural location.

THE IMPORTANCE OF CONDITION

The final factor that will affect a property's value is its condition. We live in a world where people seem to have less and less time and many buyers will not even consider a property that is in poor condition. If you have the time and imagination such properties can be a bargain – provided that you estimate the refurbishment costs accurately. We will look at how to do this in a later chapter.

CASE STUDIES

Case study 1
Sandra B bought a two-bedroom garden flat in Tooting, South-west London in January 1997. She originally wanted to buy in Balham but she could only afford a one-bedroom flat there so she settled on Tooting as the next best bet. The flat had been rented out to students and was in very poor condition. However, it had a very pretty south-facing patio garden and Sandra saw that it had potential.

Sandra redecorated the flat throughout, changed the kitchen and bathroom, laid new carpets and tidied up the pretty garden. Her work increased the value of the flat considerably. However, what really increased the flat's value was the opening of the new Jubilee Line extension in 1999. Just three years after she bought it, Sandra was able to sell her flat for more than twice what she paid.

Case study 2
Katherine C bought a two-bedroom ex local authority flat in a tower block in Dalston, East London also in January 1997. The flat was quite pleasant inside and excellent value for money but the area was rather rough. Katherine hoped it would improve. It did not.

Katherine was burgled twice and her car was vandalised three times. Public transport was poor and the journey to work took over an hour. Worst of all, Katherine found that she had nothing in common with her neighbours. After three years, Katherine sold her flat for just £2,500 more than she originally paid for it.

Commenting on her experience Katherine said 'There is no doubt that buying that flat was a mistake. With hindsight I should have bought a smaller flat in a better area. Some of my friends who bought in Islington at the same time as me have seen their flat rocket in value. I made an expensive mistake.'

3

Finding the Right Property

DEALING WITH ESTATE AGENTS

Love them or loath them, you will have to make friends with all the estate agents in your chosen area in order to ensure that you are told about all the new properties that come up for sale. When dealing with estate agents, it is important to bear three things in mind.

1. Estate agents are not on your side. Their job is to get the maximum possible price for their client, i.e. the seller.

2. Most estate agents usually have far more buyers than they have properties to sell. At the time of writing, agents in the Southeast have 13.8 buyers for every property on their books. This means that you need estate agents more than they need you. Unless you are nice to them, you will simply not get to hear about the best properties.

3. Most estate agents grade their buyers into different categories. If you want to be treated as a serious buyer, you will have to prove that you are serious. In practice this means being in a position to buy immediately with your own property under offer and your finances arranged. It also means keeping in regular touch with all the agents by telephone in order to see what new properties are available and making an effort to view suitable properties as quickly as possible. This sort of proactive approach will increase your chances of securing a suitable property enormously.

BUYING AT AUCTION

A lot of properties with development potential are sold at auction. Auctions can be quite intimidating places for the amateur and if you are seriously interested in buying a property at auction it is a good idea to go to an auction as an observer before you go to buy something. It is still possible to buy a bargain. Unfortunately, it is just as easy to make a catastrophic mistake.

If you make an offer to buy a property at auction then that offer will become immediately binding. You will have to exchange contracts immediately, pay a 10% deposit on the day and complete your purchase within the stipulated time, usually twenty-eight days. If you do not, you will lose your 10% deposit, be sued for breach of contract and be liable to pay any shortfall between the price which you agreed to pay for the property and the amount for which it is subsequently resold. You cannot therefore bid for property until you have completed the necessary preparation.

1. Do your homework on the property

You will need to arrange to view the property. If it is in need of refurbishment, you will need to take your builder or surveyor with you to estimate the likely cost of necessary work. If you are unfamiliar with the area you will need to check it out carefully (see previous chapter). Never buy a property that you have not seen, however tempting the price may seem to be. Some properties are sold at auction for what appears to be a fraction of their true value. There is nearly always a reason for this (see case study at the end of this chapter).

2. Arrange your finances

Unless you have the cash in the bank, you **must** have mortgage funds in place **before** the day of the auction. This means that you will have to apply for a mortgage, pay the building society valuation fee and have an offer of mortgage in writing before the day of the sale (see also chapter on raising the finance). The 10% deposit must be paid on the day of the sale. You should check with the auctioneers about what arrangements are acceptable to them but most require a banker's draft.

3. Instruct your solicitor

You will need a conveyancing solicitor lined up to check that there are no legal problems with the property or unfair terms in the contract of sale.

4. Decide on a maximum price

There have been many instances of inexperienced buyers getting carried away in the heat of the moment and paying far too much for a property at auction. Decide what you are prepared to bid for the property and stick to it. If you don't trust yourself to do so ask someone else to bid on your behalf.

5. Be prepared for abortive costs
If you do not manage to secure the property you are interested in, you will still have to pay your solicitor and you will not be able to recover the mortgage application fee. These abortive costs will come to several hundred pounds. You may have to bear these costs several times before you secure a suitable property.

AT THE AUCTION

On the day of the auction try to arrive in plenty of time. Many auction houses require you to register as a bidder at the start of the sale. Check whether this is the case, otherwise your bid may not be accepted. Double-check the catalogue entry – you wouldn't want to buy the wrong property by accident! It has happened!

Stories of people scratching their noses and buying a house by mistake are greatly exaggerated. The auctioneer will be watching your whole body not just your hands and he will not misinterpret who is bidding and who is not.

Try to avoid making the first bid. If a property is not popular, the auctioneer may drop the opening bid to a lower level. You wouldn't want to pay more than you had to. Once you have entered the bidding, try to pause for a second or two between bids. By slowing down the pace you can help to prevent your opponent from getting over-excited and bidding more than they intended to. Finally, do not on any account bid above your previously agreed limit.

The down side of buying at auction is the high chance of incurring abortive costs (many of your opponents will be professional dealers who will be buying for cash and able to estimate their own refurbishment costs. Their costs therefore will be much lower than yours). The up side is that there are genuine bargains to be had. The dealers will typically be looking for a margin of 20% plus financing costs. This margin can be yours – if you buy wisely.

BUYING PRIVATELY

The great majority of properties are sold through estate agents, but it is certainly possible to buy a property privately. Private sellers are not always aware of the true value of their property and bargains can occasionally be had.

There are three ways to go about finding a property privately.

- Private advertisements – most local papers have a private sellers section at the back.

- Advertise yourself. It might be worth trying your own 'wanted' advertisement in the local paper. Describe the property that you are seeking, state your price range and make it clear that you are private buyer and that no commission will be payable.

- Leaflet drop – the most successful way to find a property is to leaflet houses in the street that you are interested in. Again, remember to make it clear that you are a private buyer and that no commission will be payable.

MAKING AN OFFER

The importance of speed

In a buoyant market, properties can and do sell very quickly. Once you have seen a property that you like don't dither – make an offer as soon as possible.

Deciding how much to offer

Estate agents value properties by comparing them against comparable properties in the area. These properties fall into two categories, properties that are currently for sale in the same price range and are therefore competing for the same buyers and properties that have recently been sold where the actual price achieved is known. You need to make your assessment of the value of the property that you are intending to buy using the same method.

Before you make your offer try to obtain as many details of other properties in the area as possible. How do they compare? If you are buying a property on an estate, you may be able to find comparables that are almost identical to the one that you are considering. Valuing this type of property is relatively easy.

If you are intending to buy a more individual property, you will need to apply a number of adjustment factors to the comparable properties that are available. Some of the most important factors to take into account are:

- extensions and improvements

- condition

- area

- location.

Submitting the offer

It is best to make the initial offer in writing if possible – this will help to ensure that your offer is communicated accurately and will help to avoid future misunderstandings or disputes about who said what. In the interest of speed a fax is best.

The initial letter should:

- Be clearly marked 'subject to contract'.

- Summarise the benefits of your buying position and your timescale.

- State the price offered.

- Justify the price offered.

- List any other conditions.

See the example in Figure 1.

Handling the negotiations

The traditional process of negotiation is highly confrontational. The parties start off a few thousand pounds apart and each side takes turns to increase or decrease the price that they are prepared to pay or accept.

The problem is that each concession makes the parties more determined not to give in again and all too often the negotiations reach deadlock. Sometimes the issue left unresolved is trivial to the point of farce. Most estate agents can tell a story about a sale that did not proceed because of a dispute over a garden shed, a tired old stair carpet or even a wooden toilet seat!

The way to avoid this is to keep asking the simple questions

Dear Mr Jones,
re: 27 Avenue Gardens, Anytown
Subject to Contract

I should like to make an offer to purchase your property.

I am in an excellent position to proceed quickly. I am in
rented accomodation at the moment and I have no property
to sell. I have a large deposit and my mortgage is already
arranged. I could probably exchange contracts within four to
six weeks.

I should like to make an offer of £65,000. I feel that this is a
fair price for the property because a sale was agreed at this
figure on 17 Avenue Gardens three weeks ago. Number 34 is
also up for sale at £65,950.

My offer is subject to survey and subject to you taking the
property off the market immediately.

I hope that my offer is acceptable to you and I look forward
to hearing from you shortly.

Yours sincerely,

P SMITH.

Fig. 1.

'Why?' and 'How?' If the vendor rejects your first offer, ask them
why they have rejected it and how they have arrived at the figure
they require. The correspondence might continue as illustrated in
Figures 2–6.

The technique of asking the other party to justify their position
works like a magic charm and can be used several times during
the same negotiation.

Dear Mr Smith,
Re: 27 Avenue Gardens, Anytown
Subject to Contract

Thank you for your offer to buy our property. I am afraid
that we cannot afford to take less than £69,000.

Yours sincerely,

MR JONES

Fig. 2.

Dear Mr Jones,
Re: 27 Avenue Gardens, Anytown
Subject to Contract

I am sorry to hear that you cannot accept our offer. Before I
consider increasing it, could you tell me how you arrived at
your valuation of £69,000?

I look forward to hearing from you.

Yours sincerely,

P SMITH

Fig. 3.

Dear Mr Smith,
Re: 27 Avenue Gardens, Anytown
Subject to Contract

17 Avenue Gardens was in poor condition and required redecoration. No. 34 has no garage. I feel therefore that our property is worth £69,000.

Yours sincerely,

MR JONES

Fig. 4.

Dear Mr Jones,
Re: 27 Avenue Gardens, Anytown,
Subject to Contract

I agree that no. 17 was in poor condition and on this basis I am prepared to raise my offer to £67,000. I feel that this is a fair offer and I hope that you will now accept it. May I remind you again that we can move very quickly.

Yours sincerely,

P SMITH

Fig. 5.

Dear Mr Smith,
Re: 27 Avenue Gardens, Anytown
Subject to Contract

Thank you for your revised offer with I am prepared to
accept provided that you exchange contracts within six
weeks. Please contact my estate agent to arrange all the
final details.

Yours sincerely,

MR JONES

Fig. 6.

Competing with other would-be purchasers

Even in a quiet market, the vendors of the best properties often
receive more than one offer. The way to get your offer accepted is
to sell the benefits of your buying position to the vendor. For
example, if you know that the vendor needs to move quickly,
stress the speed with which you can move.

By finding out what the vendor is hoping to achieve and making
your buying position match these needs, you will often be able to
get your offer accepted without increasing the price.

Sealed bids

When a property is in great demand, the agent will sometimes
advise going to sealed bids. Would-be purchasers are asked to
make their best and final offer in writing by a given date. The
difficulty when deciding what offer to make is that you do not
know what the other parties have offered. If you are determined
to secure the property a good way to do so is to bid an odd
amount, e.g. £111,111. Most people bid in round figures so you
might win the contest by one pound.

When making a sealed bid, remember to include details of your buying position. The vendor is not obliged to accept the highest bid and if you are in a strong position he may decide to accept your offer even if he has a higher one.

ESTIMATING THE COST OF BUILDING WORK

If you are buying a property in poor condition you will need an accurate idea of the cost of the necessary building work *before* you make an offer. You cannot rely on your own judgement – you could be horribly wrong. You also cannot rely on your surveyor – his estimate may also be inaccurate and it will not come until after you have made an offer to buy the property. There are two viable alternatives.

1. A quantity surveyor. A quantity surveyor is a specialist surveyor who estimates the cost of building works. The Royal Institution of Chartered Surveyors (telephone number (020) 7222 7000) will provide you with a list of quantity surveyors in your area. A quantity surveyor will be happy, for a fee, to visit the property and give you a detailed estimate or a working estimate of the cost of the necessary works. This is by far the safest option.

2. Rely on a builder. The alternative is to ask a builder to visit the property with you. You may have to pay him for the time involved. However, even if you do so, his advice may not be impartial. Some builders underestimate the cost of the work involved so that you buy the property and give them the job. Once you have bought the property they will find other 'unexpected' work which bumps up the cost and eats into your expected profit margin.

CASE STUDIES

Case study 1

Toby and Catriona M were determined to buy a large family house for refurbishment in Hammersmith. They registered with every estate agent in the area and Catriona rang them all at least twice a week. Their persistence paid off when a four-storey house in need of complete refurbishment came onto the market. They viewed the house the day that it went onto the market, had their builder round that afternoon and had an offer accepted that evening.

Commenting on her experience Catriona said 'I probably made a bit of a nuisance of myself but my persistence paid off and we have bought the property that we wanted.'

Case study 2

Rupert and Charlotte W had tried to buy three properties at auction but had been outbid on each occasion. Despite being cash buyers they were finding it harder than they expected to secure the right property. They attended an auction in London in May 1998, intending to buy a repossessed farmhouse near Gloucester which had a guide price of £500,000. On the morning of the sale their eye was caught by a fantastic manor house in Shropshire. It had been repossessed by the bank and was a late entry in the catalogue. It had a guide price of £200,000. This seemed incredible value for money. On the spur of the moment Rupert and Charlotte decided to bid for it. To their delight they bought it for £170,000.

Their delight turned to horror when they viewed the property with their surveyor. The property had been partially converted into an hotel and was uninhabitable. The sheer scale of the work was enormous. However, the real problem was that the building was listed and the former owners had been served with a repairs notice ordering them to restore the building. The cost of doing this would be astronomical.

The cost of restoring a listed building of this size was beyond Rupert and Charlotte's means and they were left with no alternative but to resell the property immediately.

Local agents were unable to find a buyer and the property was eventually resold at auction six months later for just £120,000.

Commenting on his experience Rupert said 'I wish to God that we had never seen the place. All told, the cost of financing, temporary repairs, legal costs, stamp duty and the loss that we made on the property have come to more than £100,000. We should never have bought a property at auction without doing the proper research.'

Case study 3

William and Mary S bought a four-bedroom Victorian house in Brighton. The house had been used as bedsits and was in a terrible state. They knew a good local builder and asked him to give them an estimate for the cost of refurbishment. He reckoned it would be approximately £20,000. They made an offer for the property with this budget in mind.

Twelve months and £20,000 later the refurbishment was far from finished. Their eventual bill came to £37,000.

Commenting on his experience William said 'With hindsight it would have been much cheaper to buy a property in good condition in the first place. We have not made anything like the profit on the property that we intended. We really should have had more than one estimate before we committed ourselves.'

4

Raising the Finance

Taking out a mortgage is one of the most important financial decisions that you will ever make. The total cost of repaying a £100,000 mortgage over 25 years is likely to be around £225,000 and choosing the most competitive mortgage lender could easily save you £50,000 or more over the full mortgage term. A mortgage is therefore something that must be chosen with the greatest of care.

RAISING FINANCE ON A PROPERTY IN POOR CONDITION

Many building societies are reluctant to lend money on property that is in poor condition and the majority of lenders impose some restrictions. Most lenders will require you to put down a substantial deposit and many will ask you to prove that you have the necessary funds to pay for the cost of refurbishment. However, some lenders specialise in this market. Several offer staged payment loans which are ideal for the amateur property developer. The building society surveyor will agree the value of the fully refurbished property and make an offer of mortgage based on this. A percentage of the loan will be made available to buy the property. Further payments will be made as the building work progresses. Some lenders will agree in advance how much money will be released at what stage of the building work.

USING A MORTGAGE BROKER

A good mortgage broker will be able to compare the cost of a loan from all the mortgage lenders and advise on which one is best for you. However, you need to chose a mortgage broker with care. In particular you should look for:

- A broker who specialises in the mortgage market.

- A broker who can offer you products from all the UK mortgage lenders (there are more than one hundred) rather than being restricted to a panel of just a few lenders.

- Ideally a broker who can offer independent financial advice on any associated insurance policies as opposed to being tied to just one insurance provider.

(Choosing a mortgage is dealt with in far more detail in my book *Buying a House*, published by How To Books, price £9.99 ISBN 1-85703-292-6.)

FINANCING THE BUILDING WORKS

Unsecured loans

Many financial institutions offer unsecured loans of up to £15,000 which can be used to fund home improvements. The interest rates of such loans are quite competitive – typically 3–4% above the mortgage rate.

There are two drawbacks. The first is that the maximum term for repaying such loans is usually between five and ten years. This means that the monthly payment figures will be significantly higher than if the same sum were to be borrowed on mortgage. The second drawback is that the penalty for early repayment is often substantial. If you sell the property and repay the loan early you may find that the loan turns out to be an expensive one.

Secured loans

The second option is to take out a second mortgage from your own or a second mortgage lender. The advantage is that the loan can be taken out over 25 years. This keeps the monthly payments to a minimum. The drawback is that the arrangement fee can be substantial, particularly if the value of the combined loans exceeds 75% of the value of the property. At this point many lenders charge an indemnity guarantee premium to protect them (but not you) against the cost of you defaulting on your loan. The increased risk to the lender also means that the interest rates on second mortgages are usually higher than interest rates on first mortgages. A final drawback is that the penalty for early repayment is often severe.

Your own bank

The final option is your own bank. If you want a personal loan over a fixed period of time, you need to compare the interest rate and other terms on offer with the other lending sources mentioned above. However, if you only want to borrow the money for a short period of time (less than about a year) an overdraft might be the cheapest option. The main benefit of an overdraft is that you only pay for the money that you borrow and there is no penalty for early settlement. Your bank's willingness to grant you a loan will depend on your own credit history, the amount of collateral that you have in the property or in other assets and the attitude of your own bank manager to property development.

Building society retentions

A common problem when applying for a mortgage on a property in poor condition is that the mortgage lender retains part of the money until certain repairs are made to the property. For example, the survey might reveal that the roof needs to be replaced at a cost of £10,000. The lender might respond to this by withholding £10,000 from the mortgage advance until the repairs are completed to the satisfaction of their surveyor.

This can cause problems. If the lender withholds £10,000, how do you finance the necessary repairs to the roof? Fortunately this problem is usually quite easy to overcome. What you need to do is to take your offer of mortgage to your bank and ask for an overdraft facility for the retained amount. Your solicitor will give your bank an undertaking to repay this from the proceeds of the mortgage advance when it is released in due course.

CASE STUDY

David L bought a ruined Victorian barn for conversion into a four-bedroom property. The barn cost £100,000 and building works were projected to cost another £100,000. David believed that the final property would be worth at least £250,000. David approached a specialist mortgage broker who arranged a loan for £150,000 with funds released in stages. David had a deposit of £50,000 of his own.

The first payment of £75,000 allowed David to buy the property and start the building works. Further payments of £25,000 were released at stages as the building work progressed.

Commenting on his experience David said, 'The building society was marvellous. The money came in good time for me to pay the builders and I have ended up with a beautiful home refurbished entirely to my own taste.'

5

Dealing with Architects, Surveyors and Planning Consultants

Professional advice is expensive but failing to seek professional advice can be financially ruinous. My objective in this chapter is to explain what professional advice is available and give guidance on when to call in an expert.

DEALING WITH SURVEYORS

General practice surveyors
If you are buying a property with the aid of a mortgage your lender will insist on instructing a surveyor to carry out a valuation for mortgage purposes. You would be very unwise to rely soley on this report to determine the condition of the property. The purpose of a mortgage valuation is to reassure the lender that the property is satisfactory security for a mortgage. Before you commit yourself to purchasing any property, particularly one in poor condition, you need a more comprehensive survey. There are two choices.

Home buyer's report
A home buyer's report will give you much more detailed information about the condition of the property that you are buying. It is appropriate if the property:

- was built after 1919

- is of a traditional construction

- is free from obvious structural defects.

A home buyer's report is prepared in a standard format in order to keep costs down. In the year 2000 the typical cost of a home buyer's report for an average size property was around £275 plus VAT.

Building survey

A building survey is a more comprehensive report. It may be the best choice if the property:

- was built before 1919

- is of a non-standard construction, i.e. thatched or with stone walls

- is in poor condition or has obvious structural defects

- is particularly large or expensive.

The typical cost of a building survey for an average size property in the year 2000 was approximately £400 plus VAT.

Both types of report can usually be undertaken at the same time as the mortgage valuation.

Quantity surveyor

A general practice surveyor's job is to point out the defects. A quantity surveyor's job is to produce a detailed estimate of the cost of rectifying them. A good quantity surveyor can earn his fee many times over. He or she will:

- Produce a detailed specification for the necessary works.

- Produce a detailed estimate setting out what each job should cost.

- Provide guidance on how much money should be released to the builders at each stage of the works.

A quantity surveyor's 'schedule of works' will help to ensure that you choose the right builder, compare each quote on a fair basis and pay a fair price for your building work. If the work that you are contemplating is major, a quantity surveyor's report could prove to be an excellent investment.

Building surveyors

A building surveyor's job is to ensure that all your building work is completed to a proper standard and is in accordance with all current regulations. It can be extremely difficult to detect sub-standard building work and a good building surveyor can also save his fee many times over.

Structural engineer

A structural engineer has two main functions. The first is to advise on whether a property suffers from subsidence or structural movement and if so, to advise on what action is necessary to rectify the problem. Before you buy a property that shows any sign of structural movement (cracks or wonky doors and window frames) you would be well advised to have it checked over by a structural engineer.

A structural engineer's second main function is to advise on the consequences of any structural alterations to the property. For example, if you were going to demolish all or part of a load-bearing wall the structural engineer would be able to advise on what size supporting beam would be required above the new opening.

DEALING WITH ARCHITECTS

The architect's job is to advise on the design of new buildings, extensions and internal alterations. A good architect can add to the resale value of the property in many ways. For example, an imaginatively designed extension built in sympathetic materials might add many thousands of pounds to the value of property. A clumsy out-of-proportion flat-roofed extension might on the other hand actually detract from the value of some properties.

A good architect will also be able to advise on the best use of internal space. By getting an extra room out of an extension or bringing light into a dark corner, a good architect can add thousands of pounds to the value of a property.

The architect's other main job is to ensure that all proposed building works meet current regulations.

DEALING WITH PLANNING CONSULTANTS

Most internal works do not require planning permission. In most areas you are also able to extend your property by up to 10% (up to 15% if your property is semi-detached or detached) without obtaining planning permission (if you live in a conservation area different rules apply). However, the consequences of undertaking work without planning consent can be catastrophic. The planning inspector could make you restore the property to its former condition. If in doubt it is always worth contacting the local council to ask if your proposed works require planning consent.

You can apply for planning permission yourself but if the outcome of your application is of great financial importance or if the application is controversial in any way, you would be well advised to retain the services of an experienced planning consultant.

A good planning consultant will have a good working relationship with the local planning department and will often be able to advise what will be acceptable to them without making a formal application. Many of the most experienced planning consultants are members of the Royal Institute of Town Planners, (their telephone number is on page 126).

GETTING THE BEST OUT OF YOUR PROFESSIONAL ADVISERS

Many professionals offer more than one of the above services. For example, many architects offer a quantity surveying service, a planning service and a building surveying service. In my experience this often causes problems because very few people can be a jack of so many different trades. I have seen many people come unstuck because their excellent architect made a mess of their planning application, or their excellent quantity surveyor made a pig's ear of supervising their building works. My advice would be to choose separate specialists in each of the necessary disciplines or to instruct a very large firm of surveyors, architects or estate agents who have specialist staff working in each area.

CASE STUDY

Peter J owned a large four-bedroom detached house set on a 1½ acre corner plot. Several of his neighbours had recently obtained planning permission to build houses in their gardens and Peter felt sure that he could do the same thing.

He approached a small local estate agent who offered a planning service and they submitted an application to the council which was approved. The agent also put him in touch with a local builder who designed and built a four-bedroom detached house on the site at a cost of £150,000. The finished house was sold for £350,000.

Peter's feeling of contentment was spoilt three months later when his neighbour got planning permission to build *two* four-bedroom detached houses on the identical corner plot across the road and sold them for £950,000.

Commenting on his experience Peter said, 'I thought I'd done well at the time but with hindsight I could have done so much better. A more experienced planning consultant could have spotted the opportunity to build the second property and an architect would have designed a more attractive house that would have sold for a higher price. Taking the wrong advice has cost me about £350,000.'

6

Refurbishing a Property To Sell

UNDERSTANDING THE PRINCIPLES

We live in a society where many people have more and more money but less and less time available to spend it. In the majority of British households both partners now work and it is not at all unusual for both to be out of the house for 12 hours or more each day. Such people simply do not have the time to refurbish a property and many of them are prepared to pay a substantial premium for a property that is ready to move into.

The ultimate example of this is people who buy the show house on a new home site. This comes complete with all the furniture, the paintings, the ornaments and even the cutlery! By presenting a property that is in ready-to-move-into condition you will often be able to achieve a significant premium over the cost of carrying out the work. However, if you are refurbishing a property to sell it is essential that you refurbish to the tastes of your likely buyers rather than your own.

The place to start is by getting a picture in your mind of a typical buyer for your property. Think about the other people who have recently bought a property in the area. For example if you are selling a three-bedroom suburban semi your typical buyer might be a couple in their early thirties who have recently started their family or are thinking of doing so. If you are selling a one-bedroom city centre flat, your typical buyer might be a single person or a childless professional couple in their twenties buying their first home. Once you have a picture in your mind of your typical buyer, you need to make decisions about decoration and refurbishment that will appeal to as many of these people as possible.

Most people's tastes are fairly conservative. An ultra-modern stainless steel and concrete kitchen might appeal to only 10% of the potential buyers for your property, whereas neutral colours might appeal to 70 or 80% of them. The fundamental principle is that if more people are interested in buying your property, you will generate more competition to buy it and therefore achieve a better price.

DECIDING WHAT JOBS TO DO

Some improvements will increase the value of a property by many times their cost. Others will add little or no value to the property. Every property is different but here are some general guidelines.

High return

- updating the kitchen
- updating the bathroom
- redecorating throughout
- installing central heating
- replacing the carpets
- landscaping or tidying an overgrown garden
- providing off-street parking or a garage
- adding a bedroom in a sympathetic style.

Medium return

- adding a flat-roofed ground floor extension
- adding a conservatory
- loft conversions.

Low cost return

- outdoor swimming pool
- ground floor bathrooms
- double glazing
- cavity wall insulation.

Some improvements can actually reduce the value of the property. Such improvements would include.

- extensions that occupy the whole garden

- stone cladding (on most properties)
- double glazing on a period property
- removal of period features (fireplaces, decorative plasterwork, etc.).

If you are intending to live in a property for twenty years such improvements might add substantially to your enjoyment of it. However, if you are refurbishing a property to sell they should be avoided at all costs.

Why do buyers buy?

Most house buyers form their impressions very quickly. Research shows that 50% of all buyers make their final decision before they even get inside the front door! The general principle therefore is that the sooner they see it the more it matters. A fluorescent purple entrance hall might seriously reduce your chance of selling. A fluorescent purple spare bedroom would be much less damaging because most people will already have made their decision before they see it. When deciding what jobs to do the best advice is to think about what order buyers will see the house in and tackle first the jobs that they will see first.

DECORATING A PROPERTY TO SELL

In order to appeal to as many potential buyers as possible, your decorating scheme should be plain and conservative almost to the point of being bland. Plain whites and creams work best in most properties. It is surprising how many different shades of white there are and what a difference they can make to a room. Warm white with a hint of pink, yellow or apricot works well in most properties although cooler whites with a hint of blue or green can work well in a very bright south facing room. Lining papers should be plain rather than woodchip unless the plasterwork is very uneven.

Dark or heavily patterned carpets can make a room look much smaller. Changing the carpets is not prohibitively expensive and you will often recoup the cost many times over. As with everything else, plain beiges and creams work best. A small pattern or speckled effect will mean that the carpets don't show the dirt so much.

If you are updating a bathroom it is usually best to stick to a white or cream suite and plain tiles which won't date and which will go with any colour that the future owners choose to paint the room. The same advice holds true for kitchens. For most properties it is usually best to stick to conservatively styled units in neutral colours.

Different rules apply if you are refurbishing a very expensive property. Buyers of such properties will often pay a premium for an individual home and your decoration scheme may need to be more imaginative. If you have any concerns about your ability to choose a suitable scheme it may be worth retaining the services of an interior designer. A skilful designer can increase the value of a luxury home by many times the cost of their fee.

LIGHTING A HOUSE TO SELL

Lighting is often neglected. I believe that it is so important that I have given it a special heading all of its own. Lighting can completely change the appearance and atmosphere of a room in moments. Good lighting can signicantly enhance the value of a property. Poor lighting can on its own be enough to prevent a sale.

Natural light

Your first priority should be to make the best use of natural light. Have all the windows professionally cleaned, take down the net curtains, tie back heavy curtains and trim back any overhanging shrubbery. The installation of an extra window, patio door or skylight can be enough to transform a dark and unattractive room and is often a relatively cheap job to do.

Artificial light

Table lamps are cheap to buy and can transform a room. Bulbs should be 60 or 100 watt. Soft toned bulbs are better than plain glass ones. Pink gives a flattering and attractive light that works well in most rooms.

Large rooms need large light fittings with several light bulbs with a combined wattage of 200–300 watts or more. Halogen lighting is becoming very popular and gives an interesting and flattering light. Dimmer switches allow a far greater variety of lighting combinations.

PREPARING THE GARDEN

Gardens are hugely important. The front garden is the very first thing that potential buyers see and it is essential that it is tidy and well presented. Rear gardens should be designed to be low maintenance. Few people these days have enough time to maintain their gardens and a fussy high maintenance garden can be very off putting to many buyers. Patios are very popular and in summer should be presented complete with garden furniture and opened sun parasol.

Tubs of flowers and hanging baskets are easy to maintain and can do a great deal to brighten up an otherwise plain garden. One next to the front door will give your buyers a warm welcome.

CHOOSING THE FINISHING TOUCHES

A house that is decorated in cream and white can look rather bland. The way to overcome this is by the imaginative use of finishing touches. Fresh flowers can transform a room. Order fresh flowers for all the main rooms whilst your property is on the market. Pictures and ornaments can also do a great deal to brighten up a plain room. However, beware of making a room look too cluttered. One or two good quality pictures usually work better than lots of nondescript ones.

In the first couple of rooms that your buyer will see you need to go further than this. What you need is a centre piece in order to make your property stand out from the rest. For example, a real log fire or a log burning stove alight in the grate can transform people's perception of a sitting room. A table beautifully laid for a meal can transform a kitchen or dining room. A statue on the patio can transform the view of the garden. A beautiful rug can transform an entrance hall. These things will not of course be included in the sale but you are selling a lifestyle not just a house. The subconscious message is 'buy my house and you too will get a luxurious lifestyle with lots of friends who want to come to dinner'.

SETTING A BUDGET

If you are going to make a profit from your property development activities you will need to set a budget for your refurbishment programme and stick to it. Your starting point should be to determine the likely sale price of the fully refurbished property. (NB: when doing this it is important to appreciate that there is a maximum price for properties in most roads. If you live in a road that contains a hundred three-bedroom semi-detached houses worth £90–100,000 there would be little benefit in investment terms in adding a fourth bedroom to your property. It might cost £30,000 to do and add only £10,000 to the property's value. Over the years I have seen a great many people make the mistake of spending too much money on the wrong property.)

Deduct the price that you paid for the property from your anticipated resale price – this gives you your gross margin. Now deduct the profit that you want to make (commercial developers usually work on a margin of around 20% plus interest costs). The remaining figure is the budget that is available for your refurbishment programme.

The next stage is to allocate a budget to each of the jobs that you want to undertake. When doing so it is important to ensure that the budget is appropriate for the job. For example, a £2,000 replacement kitchen might add £5,000 to the value of a £70,000 property – profit £3,000. A £10,000 kitchen might only add £3,000 to the value of the same £70,000 house – a loss of £7,000.

You will need to obtain written estimates for any building works that you plan to undertake. This is dealt with in detail in the next chapter. If the cost of your proposed works exceeds your budget then you will need to make some compromises. It may be possible to do some of the jobs more cheaply. For example, you might be able to get away with keeping the kitchen units and just changing the doors and work tops. But beware. If the kitchen looks too cheap for the house or if any work is done shoddily, it may seriously damage the property's resale value.

If the budget is still insufficient you will need to decide what jobs to leave. The best advice here is leave the jobs that potential buyers won't see until later in their inspection tour and/or those jobs that have a lower cost recovery ratio. If the budget is still insufficient then you have either bought the wrong property or paid too much for it!

CASE STUDIES

Case study 1

Simon and Margaret M bought a three-bedroom semi-detached house in Luton, Bedfordshire in January 1997. They paid £70,000 for it. The house was situated in a road of 140 similar houses. Simon and Margaret spent £10,000 completely refurbishing the house and landscaping the garden. In 1998 Margaret became pregnant with their third child and they decided to spend another £25,000 building a fourth bedroom above the garage. They also added a £10,000 conservatory to use as a play room.

In the year 2000 Simon and Margaret decided that even with the extension the house was too small and decided to sell. They were very disappointed by the estate agent's valuation. Despite spending nearly £45,000 improving their property the agent felt that it was only worth £20,000 more than the unimproved houses in the road.

Commenting on her experience Margaret said, 'There is no doubt we spent too much money on the wrong property. Because ours is the only four-bedroom house in the road we were not able to recover the money that we spent on improvements. I really wish we had bought a bigger house in 1997. If we had bought a four-bedroom house then instead of extending this one we would be a lot better off. We have learned an expensive lesson.'

Case study 2

Rakesh P bought a large two-bedroom top floor flat in Islington, North London in January 1997 for £150,000. The flat had originally been converted from a large Victorian house in the early 1970s. The conversion had been badly and cheaply done and was looking very tired. The kitchen was 1970s blue Formica. The bathroom was 1970s avocado. The heating system didn't work and the walls were decorated in heavy patterned flock wallpaper with carpets in chocolate brown.

Rakesh spent twelve months completely refurbishing the place. He changed the kitchen and bathroom and managed to fit a second bathroom into the loft space. He added three skylight windows which made the living room, kitchen and main bedroom seem much bigger and brighter. He installed new central heating, modern lighting and redecorated and recarpeted throughout in neutral colours. Best of all Rakesh managed to get planning permission to create a stunning south facing roof terrace with magnificent views across to the City of London. Rakesh's total refurbishment budget came to £26,000. Fourteen months after he bought it Rakesh sold his flat for £310,000 to a young professional couple who both worked long hours in the City.

Commenting on his experience Rakesh said, 'I was able to buy a very ordinary rather tired flat and turn it into something special. The roof terrace was the most important improvement. It turned a nice flat into a unique flat and I am sure that I got the price that I did because of it. I've nearly doubled my money in a year. I am delighted.'

Case study 3

Pam and Brian S bought a three-bedroom semi-detached house in Swansea for £55,000 in January 1998 with the intention of refurbishing it and selling it for profit. The property was very old-fashioned and this was reflected in the purchase price. In good condition the house would be worth £75–80,000.

The first job that they tackled was the kitchen. Their budget for this job was £3,000 but they saw a fabulous solid wood kitchen and spent nearly £5,000. Their second job was to replace the rotten french windows with a patio door. Their budget was £1,000 but the salesman persuaded them that they might as well double glaze the whole house while they were at it and they spent £2,700. Most other jobs ran over their budgets. It seemed such a shame to buy carpets at £6.99 per metre when the ones at £12.99 would probably last so much longer. The handmade tiles in the bathroom were so much nicer than the ones from the DIY warehouse and only cost another £400. So it went on. By the time the house was finished they had spent £17,000 against a budget of £8,000. A year later the house went on the market for £84,950. Potential buyers did like the property but they were not prepared to pay such a premium and eventually it sold for £80,000. Their profit was reduced from £17,000 to £8,000 and most of this was down to inflation in property values.

Commenting on her experience Pam said, 'There is no doubt about it, we spent too much. We forgot that we were refurbishing the house to sell and started refurbishing the house to our own taste. The profit that we made was hardly worth the trouble. Next time we will do it differently.'

Case study 4

Sandra McD bought a two-bedroom flat in Nottingham in March 1998 for £40,000. It was her first home and although she planned to sell it for a profit she was also excited about refurbishing a home to her own taste. She removed both the old-fashioned fireplaces and redecorated throughout in her favourite colours, a deep crimson for the hallway, lilac for the sitting room and orange for both the bedrooms. She installed a lovely modern kitchen made from stainless steel and brass and replaced the bath with a modern power shower. In total she spent just over £5,000 and was confident of selling her masterpiece at a profit.

Against the estate agent's advice she put it on the market in January 1999 for £51,950. Despite more than 30 viewings it failed to sell. Four months later it finally sold for just £45,000.

Commenting on her experience Sandra said, 'I loved my flat but sadly no-one else did. The eventual buyer started redecorating the day after he moved in. Next time I'll stick to more conservative decor.'

7

Dealing With Builders

According to the media, most builders are cowboys who are out to rip you off by charging an exorbitant price for a shoddy job. I have not found this to be the case. In my experience, the majority of builders aim to do a fair job at a fair price. However, if building work does go wrong, the consequences can be very serious. It is important therefore to take precautions to protect yourself against the cowboy element. This chapter will show you how to do so.

DECIDING WHETHER TO EMPLOY A BUILDER

You might be tempted to save money by undertaking the building work yourself. Be careful. Your buyer might be prepared to pay a premium for a home that is in ready-to-move-into condition but they certainly won't pay a premium for work that has been shoddily carried out by an amateur DIY buff. Indeed, shoddy DIY improvements can often reduce the value of a property.

A great many jobs are much harder to do than they first look. A good plasterer, for example, makes his job look like child's play. Most amateurs will end up with a wall that looks like a ploughed field! My advice would be to stick to the jobs that you know that you can do well. Even the jobs that you can do well are often better left to the professionals. For example, you might have the skills necessary to build some fitted wardrobes but a professional carpenter will have specialist tools, the training and the experience to do a much better job in half the time. Even if you do have the ability and the tools you must ask whether you have the time, the energy or the inclination to come home from a full-time job and start work on a major building project. My advice in this area is simple. If in doubt, get a professional in.

DECIDING EXACTLY WHAT YOU WANT DONE

Before you start talking to builders you need to decide *exactly* what you want done. So many disputes between builders and their clients are caused by misunderstandings in this area.

Even if the job that you want is a straightforward one, you need to put down all the details of the job in writing. For example, if the job is to tile a bathroom in plain white tiles you will need to specify:

- who will supply the tiles

- who will supply the tile adhesive, grout and other materials

- who will pay for the hire of the tile cutting machine, if needed

- what size the tiles will be – 4", 4¼", 6", etc.

- what quality of tile will be used (specify the make if possible)

- what fully tiled means – which areas won't be tiled

- whether the radiators and sanitary ware are to be removed from the wall, or whether they are to be tiled around

- if the sanitary ware and radiators are to be removed, who will remove them, the tiler or a plumber

- if a plumber is to be used, who will organise this and who will pay the plumber's bill

- whether the wall lights and electrical fittings are to be removed or whether they are to be tiled around

- if the wall lights are to be removed, whether the tiler will do this or whether you will need an electrician

- if an electrician is to be used, who will organise this and who will pay the electrician's bill

- whether the carpets or floor covering need to be lifted – if so, who will do so and who will pay for the cost of refitting.

Unless a detailed written specification is prepared, even a simple job like this is likely to go wrong. Different builders will quote for different jobs and you will end up arguing over the unexpected extra cost of hiring a plumber, electrician and carpet fitter, or disappointed because the tiler did not tile under the washbasin.

Even a simple job like this needs a detailed written specification, setting out precisely what you want done and how you want the builder to do it. When the job involved is larger or more complicated it is often worth employing a quantity surveyor or professional building estimator to draw up a proper specification (see Chapter 5).

DECIDING WHAT TYPE OF BUILDER YOU NEED

Before you start to compile a shortlist of possible builders you have to decide what type of builder you need. Builders fall into four main categories.

Large building contractors

A large building contractor will handle the whole job for you from start to finish. They will organise all the materials, employ all the labour and supervise and coordinate the job. Many of the very large firms also employ architects and planning consultants so they are able to design new extensions, prepare the drawings, obtain planning permission and apply for building regulation approval.

The drawback is cost. When you employ a firm like this you are paying for convenience and convenience comes at a price. Such a firm will charge a mark-up on the costs of all building materials used and on the labour costs of all their own builders and sub contractors. On top of this the firm will be registered for VAT and this means that they will have to charge VAT at 17½% on the cost of the whole job. (NB: VAT will already have been charged on the costs of most building materials – you will not have to pay it twice). The result will be a bill that is significantly higher than the cost of using a smaller builder.

Small local contractors

Small local contractors have a maximum turnover of £50,000 per annum (year 2000 figures). This means that they do not have to charge VAT on their building works. Such builders will invariably work on a job themselves and arrange sub contractors as necessary to undertake the parts of the job that they cannot handle themselves. They will also arrange for the supply of building materials. However, in order to keep their turnover beneath the £50,000 limit, small contractors sometimes ask you pay for building materials and sub contractor's wages directly.

The main advantage in employing a small contractor is cost. Although he will still charge a mark-up on the cost of labour and building materials that he supplies, you will not have to pay VAT and this will save 17½% on the labour content of the job.

The main drawback is delay and inconvenience. A large building contractor might be able to send a team of a dozen workers to a job and finish it in a month. A smaller contractor might undertake most of the work himself and take six months to complete the same job.

Employing sub contractors directly

The third option is to employ the various sub contractors yourself – i.e. you find your own carpenter, bricklayer, plumber, electrician, ceramic tiler, etc. The benefit is cost. Most sub contractors are not registered for VAT. In addition to this you will save the mark-up (typically 20–30%) that small contractors levy on the cost of labour that they have supplied.

The drawback is far greater inconvenience. Many of the individual jobs will be interdependent. For example, the plasterer can't plaster the wall until the carpenter or bricklayer has finished building it and the electrician has finished running cables through it. The tiler can't tile the wall until the plaster is dry. The plumber can't hang the radiator until the tiler has finished. The carpet fitter can't lay the carpets until the plumber has fitted the radiators. Coordinating the different workmen can be hugely time consuming. It can also be expensive when something goes wrong. For example, if the carpenter does not turn up for work one day you may end up with an electrician, plumber and tiler all being paid to do nothing, or paying them compensation for lost earnings if you have to postpone them at short notice. Unless you really know what you are doing it is far easier to pay an experienced contractor to handle all this for you.

Employing sub contractors on a labour only basis

The cheapest way to do the job short of doing it yourself is to employ the contractors on a labour only basis – i.e. you order, obtain and pay for all the necessary building materials. This has a high chance of going wrong and is not for the inexperienced or faint hearted. It can be time consuming to obtain the necessary materials. It is also very easy to order the wrong thing. For example, there are several different types of sand, each of which is used for entirely different purposes. It can also be difficult to get the quantities right. For example, how many cubic metres of sand will it take to lay a thousand bricks? If you under order you may have to pay the bricklayer to stand around doing nothing. If you over order you will have to pay someone to remove the excess sand from your front garden.

A further problem is that builders have a tendency to be wasteful with materials that they have not paid for. The tiler who is on a price for the job will hunt through the off-cut pile to minimise the number of tiles that he uses. The tiler who is on a labour only contract will just cut the corner off a new one. In my experience, employing people on a labour only basis is not to be recommended unless you already know them well.

CHOOSING A BUILDER

By personal recommendation
By far the best way to choose a builder is by personal recommendation. Go through a list of everyone you know – friends, family and neighbours – and try to think of people who have had building work done during the last few years. A recommendation from a friend of a friend or a neighbour, even one that you don't know particularly well, would be a far better place to start than picking someone at random. If you have only just moved to the area be brave and knock on the door of neighbours who are currently having building work done. If you have only just bought the property another possibility is to ask your surveyor or estate agent for a recommendation.

Choosing without a recommendation
If no-one that you know can help you will be forced to take pot luck. Yellow pages is as good a place to start as any. If possible try to use a copy that is a few years old. If the firm is still in business that alone is a good sign. Don't be misled by the size of the advertisement. Very small companies often book huge advertisements and very long established firms often make do with just a lineage entry.

Firms that say that they have been established for many years are often a good place to start. Firms that are called ABC and

Sons are also worth considering. The time that the company has been established is an extremely useful safeguard. If you are looking for a sub contractor remember to look under specialist headings, i.e. carpenter, plasterer, bricklayer, etc., as well as under the main building category.

Beware of firms that are advertising in the local paper. Some reputable firms do advertise here but many of the best firms don't need to advertise because they have enough work from recommendations and other advertising. Be extremely wary of firms who drop leaflets through your door or worst of all call on you uninvited. Many of the worst horror stories involve builders who were employed because they knocked on the door.

Some firms are members of various trade organisations such as the Federation of Master Builders or the Guild of Master Plumbers. It is important to appreciate that these are primarily marketing organisations. Most do not test the competency of their members in any way. However, membership of such a body is not a bad sign and some offer an insurance backed warranty scheme in order to help resolve disputes with their members.

Above all else, make sure that the firms that you shortlist are appropriate for the work that you have in mind. The firm that refurbished your boss's £1,000,000 house will probably not be the right firm to handle rewiring your £50,000 flat. The local carpenter who did an excellent job of building your neighbour's wardrobe might make a pig's ear of your decorating because that is not his speciality.

Wherever possible you should try to use specialists. If you want to refit a kitchen a specialist kitchen fitter will often do a better job than a general carpenter because he will have highly specialised tools and may be able to do the plumbing, electrics and tiling as well as the carpentry. If you are employing a small local contractor you should pick one who trained as a carpenter if your job comprises mostly of carpentry, or a bricklayer if your job comprises mostly of brickwork.

One final point is that in my experience the older builders are often best. Most trained during the days of the official apprenticeship and will have spent five years learning how to do their job properly. Secondly, they have been around longer and therefore have more experience and more opportunity to build up a portfolio of recommendations.

OBTAINING ESTIMATES

Have your detailed specification ready and give a copy to each builder. This will help to prevent misunderstandings later on and will also ensure that each builder quotes for the same job. Have a list of questions ready to ask each builder. These should include:

- How long have you been trading?

- Who will carry out the work?

- Who will pay for materials and when will this money be required?

- Are you registered for VAT?

- When could you start?

- How long is the work likely to take?

- Will you stay on the job until it is finished?

Most importantly of all, ask whether the builder can give you the names and telephone numbers of at least two local people for whom he has carried out similar work recently.

It is important to appreciate that the builder will be interviewing you at the same time as you are interviewing him. The best builders don't usually have difficulty in finding enough work and if you come across as being too picky or difficult the builder may well decline the job by failing to send in a quote or quoting significantly above the going rate.

When the estimates arrive, don't make the mistake of choosing on price alone. If there is a significant difference in price there is usually a reason. The builders may have quoted for different jobs or used different materials. Some builders put in a low price to get the job with the objective of making their money up by charging high prices for all extras. The only exception is when a builder is desperate for the work (in which case you might ask why this is).

An excellent way to check whether a price is about right is to obtain a copy of one of the surveyors' building price guides. These list all the common jobs and give a guide for the cost of their completion. Most local libraries will have one available. Alternatively you could obtain one from the Royal Institute of Chartered Surveyors (mail order book shop telephone number on page 126).

Before you make a final decision, be sure to take up the builders' references and check so far as possible that everything that they have told you is true. For example, if they claim membership of a professional body, ring up and check that they are still a current member.

Finally, never instruct a builder without a proper detailed written estimate that specifies exactly what work will be done, when it will be completed, the price that is to be paid, the day rate that will be payable for any extras and when payment or stage payments are due. If a quantity surveyor has prepared a detailed bill of works, you should ask the builder to sign a copy of this.

SUPERVISING THE WORK

In order to avoid problems you will need to supervise the work on a daily basis. In addition to checking that the work is being carried out to a proper standard, you will need to check that it is in accordance with the agreed schedule and with any drawings. If the works require building regulation approval you will need to check that the building inspector has called to inspect each stage of the works. Failure to do this can have serious consequences. At worst the council could insist that your new extension be demolished and rebuilt again to the proper standard. Your builder should handle day-to-day discussions with the building inspector but in view of the seriousness of non compliance you need to check that the building inspector has been kept fully up to date.

If you are in any doubt about your ability to supervise your building works, you should consider employing a building surveyor to supervise the work for you (see Chapter 5).

Extras

A common cause of disputes is the cost of extras. On most large jobs it is almost inevitable that extra works will be required. In an older house, removal of the plaster work may reveal damp or other defects that could not have been foreseen. Alternatively, as the job progresses you may change your mind about what you want done or how you want it done. Sometimes your builder may just be trying it on. I have three pieces of advice to minimise such disputes. The first is to agree a detailed specification at the outset. The second is to agree a charging basis for any extras at the outset, for example any extra time will be charged at £100 per day.

The third essential is to keep an extras book and agree the cost of each job immediately. It is so difficult to remember who said what weeks after the event.

Payment

The absolute golden rule for keeping control of any job should be never pay for work until it has been done. The moment you do so the balance of power changes and an unscrupulous builder could walk away from the job and leave you out of pocket.

Established and reputable builders will have trade accounts with local suppliers so you should not need to pay for building materials in advance. The only exception to this is when you are ordering perishable materials such as turf or materials that could not be easily used elsewhere such as made-to-measure joinery.

Labour costs should never be paid in advance. However, on a large job the builder is entitled to expect stage payments on a regular basis. The timing of such payments should be agreed at the start of the job, e.g. I will pay you a £1,000 when the drive edgings are in, another £1,500 when the block paving is laid and the balance once you have built the front wall and hung the gates. You should aim never to pay more than the value of the work that has been completed and ideally a sum of at least 25% of the value of the work should be retained until the job is finished.

Unfortunately, this is sometimes easier said than done because jobs don't always go to plan. With the above job the paving blocks might be delayed which means that the builder has to build the front wall and hang the gates whilst he is waiting. Your carefully agreed payment schedule now has to be altered to accommodate this. Your objective should be to break all the jobs down into their main component stages and agree a payment for each finished stage. A quantity surveyor would of course do all this for you.

If despite your precautions you still get into a dispute with your builder, your objective should be to resolve it through discussion wherever possible – court action is very rarely the best solution for either party. A trip even to the small claims court would mean expense, frustration, months of delay and time off work for both parties. Action in a higher court could take years to resolve and become ruinously expensive.

The great majority of building problems that occur could have been avoided if only the client had spent a little extra time taking appropriate precautions at the outset.

CASE STUDIES

Case study 1

Bob and Sue Y bought an unmodernised four-bedroom semi-detached Edwardian house in Clifton, a suburb of Bristol for £275,000 in March 1998 with the intention of refurbishing and selling it for a profit. Bob and Sue were keen DIY enthusiasts and decided to tackle most of the work themselves. They worked on the house from 6 to 12 p.m. every evening and from 9 a.m. to 9 p.m. at weekends. Many of the jobs were way beyond their experience and they encountered many problems.

They laid a new patio without thinking about drainage. It flooded the kitchen and sitting room every time it rained and they had to dig it up and relay it. They knocked out a chimney breast without supporting the chimney stack above it. It fell through the roof giving them the fright of their lives and causing £3,600 worth of damage. They spent more than 150 hours refitting the kitchen. The man next door had his done in two days. A year later they sold the house for £310,000.

Commenting on their experience Sue said, 'With hindsight I wish to God we had got professionals in to do much more of the work. It was way beyond our expertise. It took far longer to do than it should have done and at times we were almost crying with frustration. Worst of all we did not get as good a price as we had hoped for the property because the estate agent said that much of the work was sub standard and most buyers would want to do a lot of it again. Next time we will do things differently.'

Case study 2

Malcolm T wanted a quote to refit his kitchen. He bought the units from a local DIY superstore and asked three local carpenters to quote for the job of installation. The quotes came in at £500, £750 and £850. Malcolm chose the cheapest quote.

Unfortunately, Malcolm had endless arguments with the fitter. He thought that the price included disposing of the old units. It did not. Malcolm had to hire a van to take them to the tip. Malcolm thought that the quote included the plumbing and electrics. It did not. The kitchen fitter didn't do plumbing or electrics so Malcolm had to delay the job for a week whilst he found his own plumber and electrician. The plumber charged him £150. The electrician charged him a further £100. For the whole of this week Malcolm's kitchen was out of action and he had to live on take-away food. Malcolm thought that the quote included tiling. It did not. Fortunately the kitchen fitter was able to do this but he charged Malcolm an extra £150 to do so. The final bill came to £900 – plus the cost of all the take-away food.

Commenting on his experience Malcolm said, 'The whole job was a disaster from start to finish. If I had been clear about what I wanted done I'd probably have picked one of the more expensive quotes and saved myself both money and a lot of hassle.'

Case study 3

Tracy and Russell S were just about to obtain building estimates to refurbish their unmodernised two-bedroom terraced house when a builder happened to knock on the door. He said that he was working in their neighbourhood and had noticed that they had slates missing from their roof. Would they like them replaced? Russell agreed to pay him £70 and he completed the job in a couple of hours.

Russell mentioned to Stan the builder that they had just bought the house and were planning to make the ground floor open plan. Stan said that he would be pleased to take on this work and quoted them a price of £1,200 to remove the wall between the two living rooms. Russell agreed and Stan started work the next day.

At lunchtime Russell received a panic stricken phone call from his wife. Stan had knocked down the load bearing wall without supporting it properly. As a result, the wall dividing the two bedrooms above had collapsed into the sitting room. Stan had disappeared. It took three months and £6,000 to rectify the damage.

Commenting on his experience Russell said, 'I wish we'd never met Stan. The job was obviously way beyond his expertise and the cost of rectifying his mistake has nearly ruined us.'

Case study 4

Julia O'D decided to modernise her late mother's semi-detached cottage before selling it. The property, which was built in 1860, had no internal bathroom and Julia decided to build a small extension onto the kitchen which, when combined with the outside toilet, would provide a ground floor bathroom. The local council said that the extension did not need planning permission so Julia retained a local builder to do the work at a cost of £8,500.

Julia's problems started when she found a buyer for the house four months later. Their solicitor asked if the extension had building regulation approval. Julia asked her builder who said no – he assumed that she had dealt with all that herself. She hadn't.

Julia was forced to apply for building regulation approval retrospectively. The council was very difficult and insisted on a number of changes to the extension which cost a further £600.

Commenting on her experience Julia said, 'I assumed my builder would know about building regulations and he assumed that I had dealt with it. Fortunately the extension did comply with most building regulations. If it had not, I might have been made to demolish it. Nevertheless, I have had to install an ugly ventilated lobby between the kitchen and the bathroom which has cost £600 and spoilt the proportions of both rooms. It has been an expensive mistake.'

Case study 5

Rubin and Rebecca C wanted their garden landscaped. They obtained three quotes and chose the middle one which was for £6,000. They agreed detailed stages when payments would be made. The builder seemed to make a nice job of things but due to delays caused by the weather the job did not go according to plan. Many jobs had to be left half finished and it became very hard to determine the value of the work that had been completed. After four weeks they had paid £4,000. At this point the builder disappeared. Rubin and Rebecca were furious but were left with no alternative but to ask another builder to finish the job. They were horrified to get a quote of £3,750 to do so.

Commenting on his experience Rubin said, 'We paid £4,000 for £2,250 of work. At this point the original builder had no incentive to finish the job so he disappeared. Next time we will be sure to pay only for the value of the work that has been completed.'

8

Dealing With Estate Agents

Congratulations – you have finished the refurbishment work. All that you have to do now to collect your profits is to sell your property for the right price. This chapter will help you to do so.

DECIDING WHETHER TO USE AN ESTATE AGENT

You could sell your property privately but an estate agent will nearly always be able to obtain a better price. The reason for this is that the price achieved for a property is determined by the law of supply and demand. If more people are interested in buying a property there will be more competition and a higher price will be achieved.

The estate agent's main job is to be an efficient net to catch all potential buyers for your property. Some will visit his offices in person. Some will be attracted by his newspaper advertising. Some will see his advertisement in the *Yellow Pages*. Some will contact him as a result of seeing a for sale board. Some will register via the Internet. Some might be passed to him by other offices. Given all these advantages, an estate agent should be able to attract several times as many buyers for a property as a private vendor. Consequently even a bad agent will usually obtain a better price for your property than you could and a really good agent will earn his fee several times over.

ESTABLISHING WHAT YOUR PROPERTY IS WORTH

Before you invite any estate agents to value your property you need to establish what it is worth. This may seem like a contradiction in terms but the fact of the matter is that estate agents' valuations are often inaccurate. Sometimes it is down to inexperience. Sometimes it is a legitimate difference of opinion. However, some agents give deliberately over-optimistic valuations because they know that this will help them to get more properties onto their books.

The only way to protect yourself against the consequences of an inaccurate valuation is to undertake the most comprehensive price research on your own behalf. The way to do this is to obtain particulars of all similar properties that are currently for sale in the area or have recently been sold. This is the process that both the estate agents and your potential buyers will use to determine the value of your property and looking at this comparable evidence will give you a very good idea of the value of your own property.

CHOOSING THE RIGHT ESTATE AGENT

Compiling a shortlist

All estate agents are not the same. The best agent in town might be able to achieve thousands of pounds more for your property than his least effective competitor. With this sort of money at stake it is worth going to some trouble to choose the right agent.

The more potential buyers an agent has on his books the better. The number of buyers that each agent has registered will be governed by the effectiveness of his marketing campaign. You should look for:

- agents with large full colour advertisements in the local papers

- agents who have a lot of for sale boards up in the area

- agents with a large office in a prominent high street position (although some successful agents are now moving to out of town sites with more convenient access and parking).

Registering a large number of applicants is not an automatic guarantee of success. In order to sell your property effectively an agent needs to persuade potential buyers to view. This is where so many agents fall down.

The only way to establish which agents offer the best standards of service is to register with each of them as a potential buyer. You will find that the level of service that you receive varies enormously. The signs of an effective agent are:

- Initial response – the telephone should be answered promptly and cheerfully.

- Rapport – the agent should work hard to build a rapport rather than just reading questions from a list.

- Qualification – the agent should establish quickly whether you are in a position to buy immediately or whether you have a property yet to sell. This will enable him to work more effectively by spending more time with his best prospects.

- Sales effort – the agent should describe a couple of suitable properties over the phone and ask you for an immediate commitment to view them. This is far more effective than just passively sending out details.

- Property details – an accurately chosen selection of property details should arrive by post the next working day. Some firms might even deliver details by hand to local purchasers. The details should be attractively presented preferably with a full colour photograph.

- Telephone follow up – the effective agent will telephone you approximately 24 hours after you have received the details and make another attempt to get a viewing appointment. Purchasers who are followed up by telephone are far more likely to view than those who are left to contact the agent themselves.

- Ongoing follow up – the effective agent will continue to telephone you at least once a week to try to persuade you to view properties that are new to the market.

- Persistence – to be effective an estate agent must be persistent. He needs to be someone who will really *sell* your property not just wait for someone to buy it. However, the effective agent should know when to give up gracefully and should never become over aggressive.

Having finished your study of all the local agents you will be in a position to compile a shortlist of agents that you wish to see. Sometimes one agent will win hands down in every category, but more often than not you will be forced to compromise. Perhaps the agent with the biggest advertisement and the most prominent office gave you very poor service as a buyer. This could be a business that is in decline. At the other end of the scale you may have received outstanding service from an agent with a back street office and sporadic advertising. Be cautious. Service is important but it cannot make up for a lack of potential buyers to sell to.

The safest choice would be to confine your list to companies who score reasonably well in both the key areas of effective marketing and effective customer service. On this basis you should select three or four agents to value your property.

Handling the valuation appointment

After the initial pleasantries the agent will probably start the appointment by asking you some questions about the background to your move. During this part of the appointment the agent will be trying to establish three things.

- How serious are you about moving?

- What is your timescale?

- Why are you moving?

The agent will then have a look at the property and give you his opinion of its value. Before you give your reactions to this figure, ask the agent to justify how he arrived at this price. He should be able to show you particulars of several other comparable properties that he has used to arrive at this figure. If he can't, give him a black mark.

If you disagree with the estate agent's figure don't be afraid to say so and show the agent the properties that you believe justify your price. The final asking price may be arrived at through discussion and negotiation but remember that the final decision is yours. The agent's job is to advise. Your job is to obtain advice from as many different sources as possible and to decide.

Assessing the agent's sales presentation

Giving an accurate valuation is one thing. Achieving that price is quite another. Your decision on which agent to instruct cannot therefore be made on the basis of the valuation alone.

Once an asking price has been agreed, the estate agent should, of his own accord, tell you more about the service that his company offers. It is best to leave the agent to highlight the key features of his service but if necessary you should prompt him in order to ensure that the following areas are covered.

1. Experience

- How long has he personally been in the business?
- How long has he worked in the local area?
- How long has he worked for his present employer?
- How experienced are the other members of his team?

2. Company background

- Who owns the business?
- How long has the firm been established?

3. Advertising

- Where does the firm advertise?
- Do the advertisements have any special features (e.g. colour photographs)?

4. Property particulars

- Does the company use colour photographs on its particulars?

5. Coverage

- Does the company have offices in other local towns?
- If so, will your property details be available there?

6. Opening hours

- What are the usual opening hours?
- Is the office staffed by full-time people at weekends?

7. Sales methods

- Are buyers usually contacted by telephone or post?
- Will the agent accompany viewings or will you be left to show buyers round yourself?

8. Qualification/security

- How does the agency check to ensure that buyers are genuine?
- How will they check that buyers can afford to buy your property before arranging an appointment?

9. Sales progressing

- What action will the agent take to ensure that your sale reaches a satisfactory conclusion?

10. Recent results

- Has the agent recently sold other properties in your area?
- How many houses do they usually sell each month? (They might not tell you but there is no harm in asking.)

11. Testimonials

- Can the agent show you testimonials from satisfied clients?

By the end of this part of the interview you will probably have a very good idea about whether you wish to instruct the agent or not. The final factor in your decision will be the commission level.

NEGOTIATING THE FEE

The maxim you get what you pay for is true for most things in life and estate agency is no exception. If you are quoted a low fee by a conventional estate agent, you must establish how he is able to undercut his competitors. On closer examination you will often find that the lower fee is financed by less advertising, fewer staff, cheaper premises or some other such economy. If this is the case you should weigh up very carefully how these economies might affect the agent's ability to achieve the best price for your property.

If you are quoted a fee that is higher than expected you should challenge it firmly but politely. You might say something like 'I am impressed by your service but your fee is ½% more than I have been quoted elsewhere. How can you justify this differential?' Faced with this sort of challenge the effective agent might try one of two approaches.

A. He might try to justify the differential by pointing out further features of his service which are not offered by his competitors.
B. He might argue that the same negotiation techniques that enable him to gain premium fee levels from his clients will also enable him to achieve a premium price for your property!

Both arguments have some merit. It is for you to decide whether you believe that superior marketing or superior negotiation techniques will indeed lead to a higher sale price but my experience is that they often do.

Most estate agents express their fee as a percentage of the selling price but there is no need for the fee to be calculated in this way. An excellent alternative is to propose a split fee. This arrangement recognises that most of the agent's skill is used to persuade the purchaser to increase his offer by the last few thousand pounds. A split fee gives an agent a much higher reward if he achieves a premium price. It works like this.

Conventional fee

Asking price	£109,950
Expected sales price	£100,000
Fee payable £100,000 x 2%	£2,000

Split fee

Asking price	£109,950
Fee arrangement	1½% of the first £95,000 and 10% of any balanced received above this figure
Price achieved	£105,000
Fee payable	

	£95,000 x 1½% =	£1,425
+	£10,000 x 10%	£1,000
Total fee payable		£2,425

In this example the agent is £425 better off, but the vendor is £4,265 better off!

This sort of arrangement gives the agent a tremendous incentive to achieve a premium price and can be an excellent arrangement for both parties.

INSTRUCTING AN ESTATE AGENT

It is usually best to instruct just one estate agent on a sole agency basis. Sole agency has four important advantages over multiple agencies:

- It is cheaper because a sole agent has a greater chance of receiving a fee and so he can afford to charge a lower rate of commission. Sole agency fees are typically 20–50% lower than multiple agency rates.

- You will usually get a better service. Agents who are instructed on a multiple agency basis are often reluctant to spend money advertising and marketing a property which might be sold to a competitor. Your property will probably get far more exposure if you instruct an agent on a sole agency basis.

- No risk of over exposure. If a potential purchaser is offered the same property by ten different agents, he may wonder what is wrong with it. There is no doubt that over exposure can be counter-productive. A sole agency will avoid this problem.

- No conflict of interest. Imagine a situation where an agent receives a low offer for your property. If he is acting as your sole agent he can safely advise you to refuse it. If he is acting on a multiple agency basis he might be tempted to try to persuade you to accept the low offer to ensure that he gets the fee, not his competitor.

FINDING A BUYER

Approving the particulars

The first thing that your estate agent will do after instructions have been confirmed is prepare the property particulars. The particulars will play an extremely important role in persuading potential purchasers to view the property. It is therefore worth going to some considerable trouble to ensure that they show the property to its best advantage.

Ninety per cent of purchasers will look at the photograph before they look at anything else. If they don't like what they see, they will reject your property out of hand. It is therefore vital to ensure that the photograph shows your property in the very best possible light. The angle that the photograph is taken from should be chosen with particular care. Most photographs show the front elevation. However, if your property looks better from another angle there is no reason why the photograph should not show the back or the side.

Getting people to view

Within the first few days the agent should send a set of particulars to every applicant he has in the price range. But sending details alone is not enough. The effective agent will also telephone each of these applicants a few days after they receive the details to obtain feedback and attempt to persuade them to view.

The advertising campaign

The advertising campaign is a very important part of the overall marketing plan. As with the particulars, the photograph is by far the most important detail. Choose it with care. If the property doesn't sell from the first advertisement it is often worth using a different photograph for all subsequent ones.

For sale boards

A for sale board is an important marketing tool. Something like a quarter of all sales are achieved due to a board. If you really want to sell your house for the best price in the shortest time then you need a for sale board.

How long should it take to find a buyer?

It is of course impossible to predict how long it will take to find a buyer. However, statistically the time when a property in southern England is most likely to sell is during the first four weeks of going onto the market. During this period the agent is able to work on all the potential buyers who have registered during the preceding months. By the end of the first month you should certainly have had a number of viewings and you may well have achieved a sale.

In northern England the market tends to operate more slowly. If you are selling a property in the north you should allow eight to twelve weeks for the initial marketing campaign to run its course.

If you have not achieved a sale within these time scales you should begin to consider the possibility that your property is going to prove more difficult to sell than you first thought. How to sell a property that is sticking on the marketing is dealt with in detail in my book *Selling your house*, published by How To Books, ISBN 1-85703-287-x.

CASE STUDY

Fiona R put her pretty two-bedroom property in Telford, Shropshire onto the market in April 2000. She had hoped to achieve around £100,000 for the property and the first two agents who came recommended asking prices of £99,950 and £102,500 respectively. Fiona was delighed when the third agent that she saw recommended an asking price of £120,000. Fiona had her doubts but the agent was adamant that he could achieve this figure so Fiona instructed him to sell the property and signed a 26-week sole agency contract. The response was very disappointing. After two months she had had just two viewings and no offers. At this point the agent admitted that his initial price might have been a little optimistic and advised a reduction to £110,000. Fiona was furious and threatened to disinstruct him. He pointed out that she had signed a 26-week sole agency contract and said that he was not prepared to release her from it. Fiona agreed to reduce the price to £110,000 but still the property generated no interest. When the sole agency agreement expired in October Fiona instructed the original estage agent at £104,950 and the property was sold two weeks later for £102,500.

Commenting on her experience Fiona said, 'I really feel that I have been had. With hindsight it was clear that the price of £120,000 was never achievable. As a result of putting the property on the market at this price I wasted the entire summer and missed a property that I would like to have bought. I am very cross about the whole affair.'

Part Two

BUYING A PROPERTY TO LET

9

Thinking it Over

According to the media, buying a property to let is a completely risk free way to make huge amounts of money. It is not. It is certainly possible to make an excellent return from investing in property to let but, as with any investment, there are risks and you need to understand these before you commit yourself.

UNDERSTANDING THE HISTORY OF BUY TO LET

In order to understand the risks of buying a property to let it is helpful to know a little about the history of private rented property in the United Kingdom.

Until the late 1960s relatively few people owned their own homes. Most people rented homes from the council, from housing associations or from private landlords. Private landlords were generally unpopular. Rents were high. Many properties were in very poor condition and worst of all tenants had little security of tenure. Landlords often exploited their tenants. The most notorious landlord was Rackman, who charged exorbitant rents for slum properties and threw his tenants out on the street if they couldn't afford to pay them.

The then Labour government decided that it had to act to curb these abuses and in 1977 it passed the Rent Act with the intention of redressing the balance between landlord and tenant rights. Maximum rents were fixed by law and tenants were given security of tenure retrospectively.

With hindsight there is no doubt that this legislation went much too far. Private landlords were incensed and the consequence was that it soon became almost impossible for private individuals to rent a property from a private landlord. This had far reaching consequences.

Young people who wanted to leave home faced a choice between waiting years to get a council flat or taking on the unwanted burden of buying their own property. People who wanted to move to a different part of the country with their jobs found it impossible to obtain temporary accommodation unless their employer rented it on their behalf. This lack of labour mobility caused serious harm to the economy. Many landlords suffered financial hardship due to the reduction in rents and many rented properties fell into a poor state of repair. Some landlords resorted to violence, intimidation and harassment in order to persuade their unwanted tenants to leave.

The law was not changed again until 1988, when the Housing Act introduced the assured shorthold tenancy. This made it possible for landlords to rent out property at a full market rent and ended the new tenant's rights to obtain security of tenure. The legislation was well intended but it did little to increase the supply of private property. There were two reasons for this. The first was that many would-be landlords feared that a future Labour government might pass further anti-landlord legislation. The second reason was that it was very difficult for landlords to borrow money to buy properties to let. A trickle of money was invested in buy-to-let property but it was not nearly enough to satisfy the demand from tenants. In most areas there were many times as many tenants as there were properties.

This situation did not change until the mid 1990s when several major mortgage lenders launched special buy-to-let mortgage schemes. These allowed private landlords to borrow up to 80% of the cost of buying investment properties at very competitive interest rates. At about the same time, returns from world stock markets began to fall. As a consequence of these two factors, money started to pour into the buy-to-let market.

For a time investment returns were very good – returns of 12–13% were not uncommon. However, by 1999 the supply of property available to rent began to exceed demand. This over supply of rented property was compounded by falling mortgage rates which meant that it became cheaper to buy somewhere. Faced with the choice of buying a flat at interest cost of £7,500 per annum or renting the same flat with a rental cost of £12,000 per annum many people, not surprisingly, decided to buy. The inevitable consequence of this imbalance between supply and demand was that rents fell. In some areas rent fell by one third between 1998 and 1999. This caused some landlords real problems. Some had taken out large mortgages at fixed interest rates of 9 or 10%. This sudden fall in rents made it very difficult for some landlords to meet their mortgage payments.

It is my opinion that the long term prospects for buy-to-let property in the UK are excellent. Nevertheless, this little blip in the market is a useful warning of how easily an investment in buy-to-let property can go wrong.

ASSESSING THE RISKS

The main risks of buying a property to let are as follows.

The property remains empty
During any period when your property is empty you will not receive rental income. It is almost inevitable that there will be some void periods – for example whilst a property is being refurbished, in between tenants or because of a downturn in the market. Void periods can be minimised by choosing the right property, careful choice of decor and by choosing an efficient letting agent. Nevertheless, it would be prudent to base your calculations on the property being empty for at least one month each year. It would also be prudent to have access to an emergency fund of at least three month's rent to draw on in case the property does remain empty for longer than usual due to exceptional circumstances.

Non-payment of rent
A tenant who was reliable and credit worthy when he moved into your property might loose his job the following day and become unable to pay the rent. You of course will still have to continue making your mortgage payments. Careful referencing of potential clients will minimise the risk of them defaulting but it cannot prevent it. Many lettings agents offer an insurance policy that will pay the rent in these circumstances and this might be worth considering, particularly if your finances are tight.

Damage to the property
Careless tenants can cause thousands of pounds worth of damage to your property. This might range from a cigarette burn on a sofa to a property being totally destroyed by flood damage. Careful choice and referencing of tenants will minimise the chances of problems in this area and insurance policies are usually available to cover the consequences of the most serious damage.

Loss of capital value

The value of properties in some areas is declining quite quickly. A once genteel suburb can become a no-go area within a few years and areas with a high percentage of rented properties tend to be more susceptible to declining property values than owner occupied areas. A loss in the capital value of your property can have a devastating effect on your overall rate of return. The way to minimise this risk is to choose the area in which you buy with care.

Tenants who refuse to leave

If a tenant refuses to leave the property at the end of the tenancy period, you will have to obtain a court order to eject them. This will typically take about three months and it is likely that you will receive no rental payments during this time. Once again careful referencing will reduce the risk of this occurring. The consequential losses caused by a tenant who refuses to leave is also an insurable risk.

Legal consequences

Your legal obligations as a landlord need to be taken seriously. Failure to comply with fire regulations or gas regulations carry particularly heavy penalties. A good letting agent will ensure that you are fully informed of your obligations in this area.

ASSESSING THE LIKELY RETURNS

Your returns will determined by a number of factors.

Gross yield

The yield is the rent received as a percentage of the property's capital value. For example:

- You buy a property for £100,000
- You receive a rent of £10,000
- The yield is £100,000 ÷ 10,000 = 10%.

In 1999 the average gross yield from buy-to-let properties was around 9%. However, gross yields vary hugely from area to area and property to property. A large detached house might achieve a yield of only 5% whilst a small flat in a popular area might achieve 10% or more. How to choose a property that will give you the highest yield is dealt with in Chapter 10.

Increase in capital value

The rate at which your property increases in value will have a huge impact on the total return that you achieve. For example, in 1999 gross rental yields were around 9% but the average increase in house prices was 13% giving a total return of 21%. For the reasons that I explained in the last section, properties in different areas will appreciate at different rates. During 1999 house prices in some areas increased by more than 30%. In other areas they actually fell. You must take this into account when deciding where to buy your investment property.

Agency fees

If you choose to use a managing agent (see Chapter 12) you should expect to pay a management fee of around 15% of the rent received plus VAT – i.e. if the monthly rent is £1,000 you would expect to pay £150 plus VAT. This would have the effect of reducing a gross yield of 8% to a net yield of 6.8%.

Repairs and maintenance

The cost of maintenance must be taken into account. An older property is likely to cost more to repair than a newer one. This should be taken into account when deciding what type of property to buy. If you are letting the property furnished you will need to allow for the cost of wear and tear on the furniture.

Taking all these factors into account a typical return for modern unfurnished property might be calculated thus:

- purchase price £100,000

- rental income £8,000

- managing agent's fee £1,200

- repairs and maintenance £1,000

- net income £5,800, i.e. 5.8% yield

- add 8% rise in property values = £8,000

- total return £13,800 = 13.8%.

This is intended only as an example. The figures vary hugely from area to area, property to property and year to year. However, the experience of most buy-to-let investors during recent years is that the returns have compared well to the returns available from the stock market.

NB: You can increase the yield hugely by gearing up your investment, i.e. borrowing some of the purchase price (an example of how gearing can affect the yield is given in Chapter 13).

RAISING THE FINANCE

One of the attractions of buying a property to let is that it is now relatively easy to obtain the money to finance an investment. Many of the major mortgage lenders will lend up to 80% of the purchase price on attractive terms. Repayment periods can be up to 25 years and the interest rates are close to the rates charged on normal residential mortgages.

Most lenders calculate how much they are prepared to lend according to the rental income that you expect to achieve rather than basing the loan upon your own salary. This makes it easy for ordinary people to borrow large sums of money to fund the purchase of several buy-to-let properties.

Some would say that obtaining mortgage finance to fund investment in buy-to-let property has become too easy and I have some sympathy with this point of view. Those who are wholly dependent on their rental income to service their loans must have access to an emergency fund in case something goes wrong. Nevertheless when things go right, gearing up the investment in this way can produce spectacular returns.

INVESTOR PROFILES

Residential property has proved to be an appropriate investment for people from a great variety of different backgrounds. Here follows a selection of typical investor profiles.

1. Home owners who couldn't sell
A lot of people who became landlords between 1988 and 1998 did so because they could not sell their home due to the recession in the housing market.

2. Temporary job move

A lot of people who take up a temporary position in another part of the country or abroad rent out their home whilst they are away.

3. Student accomodation

Parents often find that it is cost effective for them to buy a property for their student children to use whilst they are at college. By renting out the extra rooms their off-spring can often get free accommodation. Many parents keep the property on for many years after their own children have left college.

4. Income in retirement

Buying a property to let can be an excellent way to turn a lump sum into an income during retirement.

5. Get rich quick

The ease with which mortgage money can be obtained means that people who are willing to take the risk can acquire large property portfolios quite quickly (see case study).

6. Self-invested pension schemes

Many self-employed people have a lot of money invested in their own self-invested pensions schemes. However, money from a SIP can only be invested in commercial property.

7. Retirement planning

A great many people have become disillusioned with personal pensions. The investment performance of many schemes has been disappointing and charges are high. It is impossible to get at the money before retirement age. Worst of all the fund has to be used to purchase an annuity on retirement which is inflexible and currently offers a poor rate of return. Even once the loss of tax benefits has been taken into account many people believe that buying a property to let can offer a better and more flexible vehicle for retirement planning than a personal pension plan.

8. Vehicle for tax avoidance

Many property developers retain the last few properties on a new development to rent out. By reinvesting their profit in this way they can delay paying tax.

9. Balancing an investment portfolio

People with large investment portfolios like to spread their risk by investing in different areas. An investor with a lot of money in the stock market might see an investment in residential property as a hedge against a future fall in share prices.

10. Safe haven

Many people, particularly older people, see property as less volatile than the stock market and are prepared to trade investment returns for security.

There are many more reasons why people choose to invest in residential property but the above profiles will, I hope, demonstrate how flexible an investment in this area can be.

Whatever your reasons for considering an investment in buy-to-let property, the two most important questions to ask are what is the worst that could possibly happen and could I cope with that happening to me. Provided that you fully understand the risks, buy-to-let property is an excellent investment that can meet the needs of a wide range of investors.

CASE STUDIES

Case study 1

Sean C was a young man with a lot of ambition. He moved from Norfolk to London to take up a job as a sales manager but he quickly became convinced that property offered him a fast track to the wealth that he craved. He bought his first buy-to-let property at the age of 26 in January 1995. It was a two-bedroom ex-council flat in a tower block in south-west London. It cost him £50,000. Sean obtained an 80% mortgage (£40,000) and borrowed £5,000 from his bank (he told them it was to buy a new car). He borrowed the balance of £5,000 from his father. He rented the flat out to three students at the local polytechnic. They paid him £200 per month each. This worked out to £600 per month or £7,200 per annum – a gross yield of 14.4%. Much encouraged, Sean bought a second flat in the same block two months later. Again he paid £50,000. He raised £40,000 on a mortgage, £3,000 from his employer (for a 'season ticket loan'), £3,000 from his father and put the rest on his credit card. Within six months Sean had saved enough money to buy a third flat. This time he bought a large but rather tatty flat above a shop half a mile away. It cost him £60,000 but he was able to put four more students in, each paying £200 per month – a gross yield of 16%.

A year after he bought his first flat Sean asked an estate agent to value it. He was delighted to find that its value had increased by 20% to £60,000.

Sean remortgaged it and the other one in the same block. By doing so he was able to raise another £20,000 in cash which he used as the deposit to fund the purchase of two more flats on another council estate nearby. One cost £55,000 and the other £60,000. Sean put three tenants into both of them, all paying £220 per month – a gross yield of 13.8%.

As the value of each of his properties increased Sean re-mortgaged it to fund the deposit on another property. By 1999 Sean owned 15 flats together worth around £1.5 million. The value of his outstanding mortgages was just £900,000 – a net gain of £600,000 in just four years.

Commenting on his experience Sean said, 'In the early days I knew I was sailing close to the wind but I had no dependents and nothing to lose. My investment has worked out wonderfully well. Apart from a few arguments about stained carpets and torn wallpaper, my investments have been remarkably trouble free. Buy-to-let has served me well.'

Case study 2

Yvonne and Alistair Y were planning to sell their two-bedroom flat in Brighton in January 1995 for about £60,000. They planned to buy a three-bedroom semi-detached house nearby for £100,000. However, Yvonne read a magazine article about buy-to-let property and after some discussion they decided to keep their flat to rent out and raise a larger mortgage to purchase their next property. They had £20,000 of collateral in their flat, enough to fund a £12,000 deposit for the buy-to-let mortgage and after costs to put a 5% deposit on their next property.

Over the next five years things went extremely well. The flat was let out easily and achieved a gross yield of 11.1% over the period – more than enough to pay their mortgage. However, the real bonus was that property prices in their part of Brighton more than doubled during the period. By January 2000 their flat was worth £130,000.

Commentingon her experience Yvonne said, 'I am so glad that we did not sell our flat. Renting it out has been no trouble at all.

The mortgage has been fully covered by the rent and we now own a flat worth £130,000 with a £52,000 mortgage. It couldn't have worked out better.'

Case study 3

Eileen and George D sold their family home for £400,000 in January 1998 and bought a brand new luxury sea-front flat for £100,000. George and Eileen were both 70 years of age and they considered using the balance of £300,000 to buy an annuity which would supplement their pension during their retirement. However, the rate of return was not particularly attractive and Eileen and George also wanted, if possible, to leave some money to their children.

Instead they decided to invest the proceeds in buy-to-let property and bought three other flats in the same block as their own. They had no difficulty finding tenants for their properties, each of whom paid a rent of £7,000 per annum.

Commenting on his investment decision George said, 'We are very happy with our investment. We get an additional income of about £17,000 per annum net of fees and the flats are appreciating in value as well. With hindsight we might have got a better return by buying six £50,000 flats elsewhere. Nevertheless, we like this development and we like to be able to keep an eye on our investment.'

Case study 4

Tom J bought his first buy-to-let property in January 1998. He paid £70,000 and funded his purchase with a £56,000 mortgage plus £14,000 which represented his life savings. Initially things went well and Tom was able to buy three more flats. The net rent just about covered his mortgage payments.

In January 1999 one of Tom's flats fell empty and the agent was unable to find him a new tenant. Tom lost two months' rent then dropped the rent by 20% to find a tenant.

In March 1999 a second flat fell empty and wouldn't let. Tom lost another two months' rent and eventually had to let it for 25% less than the previous rental. It seemed as if the bottom was falling out of the local rental market.

By November 1999 Tom was in serious financial difficulty – his rental income had fallen from £28,500 per annum to just £19,000 per annum. This was less than his mortgage payments and Tom could not afford to make up the difference from his salary.

The final straw came when Tom's third flat was empty for two months over Christmas. Tom missed his January mortgage payment and the building society threatened to repossess all his properties.

Commenting on his predicament Tom said, 'I am in danger of losing everything. Rents have fallen by 30% and this leaves me unable to make my monthly payments. There is a very real risk that I will end up being made bankrupt. I should never have got myself in so deep.'

10

Finding the Right Property

A great many buy-to-let investors reduce their returns because they choose an inappropriate property. If you are buying as an investment it is essential to choose a property that will have a broad appeal to tenants rather than one that you personally would like to live in. It is also important to choose a property that matches your investment objectives. This chapter will show you how to do so.

DECIDING UPON YOUR PERSONAL INVESTMENT OBJECTIVES

Different investors have different investment objectives. For example, one investor might be buying a property to let in order to boost his income in retirement. Another might earn a large salary and be looking primarily for capital growth in order to fund his retirement in many years' time. These investors would need to buy very different properties.

Before you decide what sort of property to buy you need to decide whether you are looking for the highest possible yield, the best chance of capital growth or a balance between the two. Generally speaking there is an inverse correlation between yield and capital growth. The properties that achieve the highest yield have the worst chance of capital growth and visa versa.

CHOOSING AN AREA

The majority of private buy-to-let investors buy property in the town that they live in. There is absolutely no reason to do so. If your property is going to be managed by an agent there will seldom be a need to visit, so convenience is not really an issue. The reward for any inconvenience associated with owning a property some distance away might be a substantially higher investment return. My advice on choosing an area would be to base your decision on your investment priorities rather than geographical proximity.

Investors seeking the best yield

If the objective is to achieve the maximum yield you should consider buying a property in a less desirable area. For example, a three-bedroom ex-council house in a northern university city might cost £36,000 and accommodate three students each paying £60 per week. This gives a total rental income of £9,000 per annum (£60 per week = £3,000 per annum times 3 tenants = £9,000 per annum). This represents a yield of 25% – three times the national average.

However, before you rush off to buy such a property you need to take into account several other factors.

1. Capital growth

Property in many inner city areas is actually declining in value. This erosion of capital values could significantly reduce your long term return.

2. Maintenance

Students can be rather exuberant and wear and tear on such a property might be higher than average.

3. Reliability of payment

Students are statistically more likely than most tenants to default on their rent.

4. Hassle

Such a property might be more trouble to manage than most.

Investors seeking maximum capital growth

If you are looking for capital growth you should confine your property search to the more desirable areas. For example, in the best areas of central London yields might only be around 5%. However, the value of central London properties has soared in recent years. In some areas the rate of appreciation has been more than 30% per annum. This more than makes up for the low yield.

In between these two extremes there are infinite variations. Before you choose an area you need to decide what balance you wish to achieve between yield and capital growth.

CHOOSING A PROPERTY

Your choice of property will dramatically affect your overall rate of return. Generally speaking, smaller and cheaper properties achieve better yields than larger and more expensive ones. If you have £100,000 to invest you would almost certainly get a better return by buying two flats for £50,000 each rather than one house for £100,000.

Whatever type of property you choose, it must be a property that will appeal to prospective tenants. A pretty thatched cottage with a huge high-maintenance garden situated 15 miles from the nearest railway station might be a wonderful place to retire to but it is not likely to appeal to most prospective tenants. In order to choose the right property you need to get into the mind of the person that you are trying to attract and see the property from their point of view. Here are three typical examples.

The professional tenant
The professional tenant tends to be young and single or married without children. They often work long hours and have little time to maintain their home. Most will therefore be looking for a modern low-maintenance flat located in a city centre development or in a suburb with a good rail link into town. They tend to eat out a lot so restaurants and leisure facilities are important to them. Gardens are a big turn off because they do not have the time or the inclination to look after them.

The company let
The attraction of the company let is reliability of payment. The second advantage is that agreements are often longer. One to two years is commonplace rather than the six months that most private tenants tend to sign for.

If you are seeking to attract a company let you should consider buying a property close to a hospital or a major local employer which is moving staff in and out of the area on a regular basis. London is particularly attractive because there are so many inter-national companies that regularly bring staff over from abroad.

The student let
Students want as much space as possible for as little money as possible. A big Victorian terraced house might be a good buy. The property needs to be as close as possible to the university in order

to minimise transport time and costs and within easy reach of the local night life. It doesn't matter if the area is a bit run down but it should not be dangerous.

OBTAINING ADVICE

Some of the large national chains of letting agents offer potential investors advice on choosing an area and have data on the typical yields that are being achieved in various locations.

Once you have decided on an area you should approach the local letting agents and ask for their advice on what type of property there is currently a demand for. They should be very pleased to talk to you as a potential investor. However, you should be aware that from the agent's point of view few such conversations lead to business. The agents might therefore be reluctant to spend too much time with you on a speculative basis. If this is the case it might be worth paying a local agent for an hour or two of advice. Buying the right property could transform your investment return and paying for an hour's professional advice might prove to be one of the best investments you have ever made.

FINDING THE RIGHT PROPERTY

Once you have decided exactly what sort of property you want, you will need to find it. Some lettings agents offer a finder's service where they will charge a fee (typically 1½–2% plus VAT) to search the market and find you a suitable property. This may be worth considering. However, most people buy directly through an estate agent. Getting the best out of an estate agent was dealt with in Chapter 8. If any of the local estate agents that you register with have a property management department you should mention that you are buying a property to let – it may get you priority treatment.

CASE STUDIES

Case study 1
Norman and Katy C had £200,000 to invest in buy-to-let property. They had intended to buy two or three properties to rent out to

students but one of the estate agents sent them a charming thatched cottage in the same price range and they fell in love with it. They bought it with a view to letting it out for 20 years then living in it once their children left home.

Their investment did not perform well. The cottage was very isolated and consequently proved difficult to let. The average rent achieved during the first three years was £11,000, representing a yield of just 5.5%. This was further eroded by the high cost of maintaining the property. Their net yield was a miserable 3%.

Commenting on their investment Norman said, 'Some of our friends who bought a house to rent out to students have achieved a net yield of 12%. We have achieved just 3%. With hindsight we should have bought a more conventional investment property instead of the home that we wanted to retire to. We are now planning to sell the cottage and buy somewhere that gives a better rate of return. It has been an expensive mistake.'

Case study 2

George and Edith V sold their newsagents shop and bought two two-bedroom ex-council flats in a tower block in East London for £80,000 each. Their objective was to supplement their pension in retirement. They agreed a rental that gave them a net yield of 10%, i.e. £16,000 per annum.

Commenting on their investment Edith said, 'I am not sure how values are going to hold up in this area in the long term but for the time being our investment suits us just fine. We get a far better income than we'd get from keeping the money in the building society and as basic rate taxpayers we only pay tax at 23%, giving an after tax income of £12,320 per year. This makes all the difference between a comfortable retirement and living on the bread line. It's been an excellent investment so far.'

Case study 3

Andrew T earned over £60,000 per year and wanted to invest in a buy-to-let property to fund his retirement in thirty years' time. On the advice of a local letting agent he bought a two-bedroom ex-council flat in a tower block for £30,000 and rented it out to two nurses for £120 per week, giving a total income of £6,000 per annum – a gross yield of 20%. After maintenance and agent's fees the net yield was still 14%.

Initially Andrew was very pleased with his investment but his pleasure didn't last. The first problem was that the property was declining in value. A year after he bought it the flat next door sold for just £27,000 – a fall of 10%. The second problem was that Andrew had to pay tax on his net profit from renting out the flat at his highest marginal rate of 40%.

Commenting on his experience Andrew said, 'I am receiving a net rental after expenses of £4,200 per annum. My tax bill on this last year was £1,680. However, because of its declining value I am only really getting a return of 4%, i.e. £1,200 per annum. This investment simply doesn't stack up for me. I am going to have to sell this property and buy one which achieves a lower yield but has a better prospect of capital growth.'

Case study 4

Graham B also bought a two-bedroom flat in central London for £200,000. He bought his in September 1992. However, unlike Samuel he had to borrow 80% of the purchase price on mortgage. He arranged a fixed rate mortgage at 8.75%.

Unfortunately the rental that Graham received for the flat was much less than he expected and he found it very difficult to make up the shortfall from his salary. By 1994 the net yield had fallen to 5%, leaving Graham with a shortfall to find of £625 per month. Graham was forced to sell. He got £240,000 for it.

Commenting on his experience Graham said, 'My investment was not a disaster but it could have been so much better. I predicted the rise in central London property prices, which was why I bought a property there. Unfortunately I missed out on most of the gains because I did not predict that rents would fall and I couldn't afford to keep the property. With hindsight I would have been much better off buying a flat with a rent that covered my mortgage payments even if this meant less prospect of capital growth.'

11

Refurbishing a Property to Rent

A well presented property will let more easily and command a higher rent. This chapter will cover how to present your property to its best advantage.

IDENTIFYING YOUR PROSPECTIVE TENANT

When choosing the decor, the place to start is with the prospective tenant that you are trying to attract. A one-bedroom flat in a smart city centre developement is likely to appeal to a youngish tenant. Such a person will probably prefer clean light modern furniture to heavy antiques and clean white and pastel shades to heavy flock wallpaper and patterned carpets. You should decorate accordingly.

A big Victorian house in a university town is likely to appeal to students. They might be intimidated by white carpets and sofas and may reject such a property for fear of future arguments over damage.

Tenants from overseas, particularly Americans, are famous for demanding power showers and the latest fridges, freezers and washing machines. A good letting agent will be able to give advice on what will appeal to tenants in your local area but the place to start must be to visualise the tenant that you have in mind.

DECORATING A PROPERTY TO LET

Most of what I said in Chapter 6 also holds good when you are decorating a property to let rather than sell. In order to appeal to as many prospective tenants as possible, it is usually best to stick to whites and pastel colours. However, when decorating an investment property it is important to decorate with durability in mind. Emulsion is easier to patch up than wallpaper. Patterned carpets show the dirt less than plain ones. Careful choice of decor will help to prevent you becoming embroiled in lengthy arguments about the cost of repairs.

In order to let easily most properties will need a modern kitchen and bathroom. If you are changing a bathroom it is usually best to stick to white sanitary ware in a durable finish. Plastic scratches easily. Enamel is easily damaged by the wrong cleaning materials. Kitchens should be plain and hardwearing. Slate or tiled work tops are much more durable than wood or Formica.

FURNISHING A PROPERTY TO LET

The majority of landlords now offer their properties on an unfurnished basis. There are two reasons for this. The first is that the cost of furnishing a property is often not reflected in the additional rent received . The second is that recent legislation has placed heavy burdens on landlords. For example, all furniture in a rented property now has to comply with modern fire regulations.

However, certain types of property, such as student properties, will not attract a tenant unless they are furnished. A good agent should be able to advise you on whether your property needs to be furnished and the likely rent that it will command on a furnished versus unfurnished basis. However, my advice in most cases would be to offer your property unfurnished if possible. You will however need to provide white goods, i.e. fridges, freezers, washing machines, dishwashers, cookers, etc. These are quite expensive and awkward for tenants to transport and most tenants expect them to be provided. If you are supplying electrical goods you will need to have them safety tested once a year.

For luxury properties different rules apply. Very expensive properties, particularly those in central London, are often offered on a fully furnished bais and command returns that justify this. If you are letting such a property you need the advice of a specialist letting agent.

CASE STUDIES

Case study 1

Claudia T bought a two-bedroom flat in Hammersmith. The flat was a bity 'tatty' but Claudia did not have enough money to do it up and felt that it wouldn't really matter. It took eight weeks to find the first tenant and nine weeks to find the second. Seventeen void weeks out of the first year made a big hole in Claudia's projected income.

When the second tenant left Claudia borrowed some money to refurbish the flat. She decorated it throughout, changed the kitchen worktops and cupboard doors, updated the bathroom and bought new carpets and curtains. Her efforts paid off when she found a tenant for the refurbished flat within a week at a rental of £50 per week more than previously.

Commenting on her experience Claudia said, 'My refurbishment costs will be recovered within 18 months. I wish I had spent the money refurbishing the flat as soon as I had bought it.'

Case study 2

Gordon H had orginally planned to offer his Victorian house in Nottingham on an unfurnished basis. However the letting agent said that in order to appeal to the student market the property would have to be furnished. Gordon bought the cheapest furniture he could find, mostly from small advertisements in the local paper. When Gordon asked the letting agent to call to inspect the property again he got a nasty shock. Much of the furniture that he had bought didn't meet the fire regulations and had to be thrown away. His agent also said that many of the remaining items were so horrible that even students wouldn't be prepared to live with them. Gordon was forced to spend another £2,500 refurnishing the property.

Commenting on his experience Gordon said, 'When I was a student we were grateful for whatever accomodation we were given. I can't believe how things have changed. The fiasco over the furniture has made a big hole in my first year's income.'

12

Finding a Tenant

SETTING THE RENT

It is very important to ask a realistic rent. If you ask too much the property will remain empty and this will dramatically reduce your overall return. Consider this example.

Property A

- Property let immediately at £100 per week for six months.

- Total rent received = £2,600 for 26 weeks, i.e. £100 per week.

Property B

- Takes four weeks to let at £110 per week.

- Total rent received therefore is £2,860.

- However, because there was a delay in finding a tenant this has to be averaged over 30 weeks, i.e. £95 per week.

Another factor to consider when setting the rent is that less desirable tenants may be prepared to pay higher rent. For example, three young men sharing might be prepared to pay more for a house than a young couple. However, shared tenancies tend to cause more wear and tear on the property and there is also a higher statistical chance of the tenants defaulting on their rent. Sometimes you need to make a trade off between the quality of the tenant and the amount of rent received.

The best way to establish a realistic rent is by looking through your local paper to find properties that are similar to your own.

DECIDING WHETHER TO USE A LETTING AGENT

A condition of most buy-to-let mortgages is that the property must be managed by a managing agent. Most of the mortgage lenders go further and insist that the managing agent is a member of the Association of Residential Lettings Agents (ARLA). This condition is imposed because the lenders know from experience that a good agent will significantly cut down the risk of something going wrong with the tenancy.

If you are buying an investment property for cash you could decide to handle the letting of it yourself. However, I would advise you against doing so. A good agent will add value at every stage of the process. By finding a better tenant, negotiating a higher rent and avoiding subsequent problems a good managing agent could earn their fee several times over.

Let versus full management
Most lettings agents offer three kinds of service.

Let only
This means that the agent will find a tenant, check their references and move them in. Thereafter it will be the landlord's responsibility to collect the rent, manage the property and deal with all repairs. The typical cost of a let only agreement is around 10% of the rent agreed plus VAT. It is usually payable in one lump sum at the start of the tenancy. A further fee is often payable if the tenant renews the agreement.

Let plus rent collection
The agent will find a tenant as above but will also collect the rent on your behalf. However, you will be left to look after the property and to arrange any necessary repairs. The typical cost of the rent collection agreement is about 12½% of the rent plus VAT.

Full management
The agent will find a tenant and collect the rent as above. However, with a full management agreement they will also look after the property and arrange all necessary repairs. The typical cost of the full management agreement is around 15% of the rent plus VAT.

Most landlords go for the full management option. It is a condition of most buy-to-let mortgages and most other investors find that the convenience is worth the cost.

CHOOSING A LETTING AGENT

Many good estate agents offer a rotten property management service. The reason for this is that they dabble in the lettings market and do not have enough properties on their books to justify investing in the specialist systems and staff necessary to run an efficient operation. When choosing a managing agent it is essential to choose a firm that specialises in the lettings market.

Compile a shortlist of firms by looking for those with the biggest advertisement in the local paper. You might also consider registering with each firm as a prospective tenant in order to test out the level of service that they offer. On this basis you should select a shortlist of two or three firms to invite to see your property.

The valuation appointment itself will be very similar to the estate agent's appointment described in Chapter 8. The agent should start by talking to you about your needs and priorities and then give you his opinion on what rent he believes he can achieve for the property. A good agent should be prepared to justify his recommended rent by showing particulars of similar properties that have been let or are currently available in the immediate area. The agent will then move on to their selling presentation.

Here are some questions that you might ask at this stage:

- How long have you been established?
- Are you a member of the Association of Residential Letting Agents?
- How many properties do you have under management?
- Do you work full time in the lettings market?
- How many staff work for the lettings department?
- How will you go about finding a tenant?
- How many tenants do you have for my property at the moment?
- How do you go about referencing a tenant?
- Do you offer an insurance scheme that guarantees rent if the tenant defaults?
- Which major local companies do you act for?

- Do you have a separate property management department?

- Is your property management system computerised?

- Do you offer an inventory service?

- How often will you visit the property?

- Can you provide me with a statement of account that is in a format that is acceptable to the Inland Revenue?

- Why should I instruct you rather than your competitors?

Instructing a lettings agent

Most lettings agents are prepared to work on a multiple agency basis. However, if the agents are competing with each other to earn a fee there is danger that you will be put under pressure to accept the first tenant for the property rather than the best tenant that is available. It is usually best therefore to instruct just one agent on a sole agency basis. If they don't find a tenant within a reasonable time you can always sack them and instruct another.

Negotiating a fee

For many years managing agents charged 15% for a full management service 12½% for rental collection and 10% for let only. However, today there is a huge variation in the fee charged by different firms.

It is not always easy to make direct comparison because the fees charged by different firms are calculated on a different basis. Some firms charge a set-up fee for preparing the contract. Some charge for preparing an inventory. Some charge a mark-up on the cost of all repairs that are required. Some charge a fee if the tenant renews the agreement. The best way to ensure that you are comparing like for like is to ask each agent for a written quote or summary.

However, you need to be very cautious about choosing a lettings agent on the basis of fees alone. A tenancy that goes wrong can cost thousands of pounds in repairs, lost rent and legal fees and paying a few pounds per month extra to retain a reputable lettings agent could prove to be an excellent investment.

FINDING A TENANT

The lettings market moves much more quickly than the estate agency market. Most lettings agents telephone prospective tenants rather than sending out details. Indeed, many lettings agents don't prepare written details at all.

Your agent should have a list of prospective tenants in each price range and they should telephone these people to arrange a viewing as soon as they receive instructions. Most tenants make their minds up very quickly and want to move in immediately. It is therefore not at all uncommon for a property to be let within a few days of it becoming available.

If the agent doesn't have a suitable tenant on his books your property will have to be advertised. You should expect it to be advertised each week until a tenant is found.

If a tenant has not been found within a reasonable period (two to three weeks) you should consider instructing other agents. Many agents have special relationships with large local employers and it is not at all unusual to find that agent B finds a tenant immediately even after agent A has failed.

If the property is still not let after about a month you will need to find out why. Ask the agent for detailed feedback from people who have seen the property and decided not to take it or decided not to view it at all. Ask also to see particulars of the properties that you are competing with. If you can't find any obvious reasons for the property sticking the only remaining option is to reduce the rent.

REFERENCING A TENANT

Thorough referencing of the tenant is the best protection you have against future problems. Your agent should ask the prospective tenant to fill out a comprehensive application form and check the accuracy of every answer. In particular they should take up:

- Credit references – an on-line search with a credit agency will show whether the tenant is credit worthy and whether they have any county court judgements for debt.

- Employment references – a reference from their employer will help to confirm that the tenant is in secure employment and can afford the rent.

- Personal references – a reference from, for example, a previous landlord will help to reassure you that the tenant will respect the property and leave it in good condition.

Many lettings agents contract out the referencing process to specialist companies. Many firms now also offer an insurance backed warranty that covers the landlord against losses incurred in the event that the tenant defaults on the rent, causes damage to the property or fails to leave at the end of the tenancy period. Such schemes are well worth considering.

If there is any doubt about a prospective tenant's references my advice would be to decline the tenancy.

DSS tenancies

A great many landlords and lettings agents now refuse to let properties to tenants who are claiming housing benefit from the department of social security. This is a great shame. Many individual claimants are honest people who have fallen on hard times through no fault of their own. However, in recent years the government has introduced a number of rules which are grossly unfair to landlords. For example, if it is found that the tenant was claiming benefit fraudulently, the DSS may reclaim all rental monies paid to the landlord. The landlord is not in a position to know whether a claim for benefit was fraudulent and it seems grossly unfair to reclaim money from an innocent party. Under the present rules my advice would be to steer clear of DSS tenancies.

CHECKING IN THE TENANT

Most agents ask for a month's rent as a deposit to cover the cost of minor damage. However, in order to avoid future disputes it is important to create a detailed record of the condition of the property at the start of the tenancy. The easiest way to do this is to create a photographic record of the condition of each room.

If the property is to be let on a furnished or part furnished basis you will need to prepare a detailed inventory listing every item in the property down to the last teaspoon. Most lettings agents will do this for you although most charge a separate fee to prepare an inventory.

Many experienced landlords try to meet each of their new

tenants at the start of the agreement. Their theory is that people will take better care of a property if they know the owner. My experience is that there is a lot of truth in this and if possible you should try to meet all your tenants at the start of their tenancy.

AVOIDING PROBLEMS

If you've appointed an agent on a full management basis they should visit the property every three months or so to check that it is being properly cared for. In between times a useful safeguard is to walk past the property yourself to check that everything is as it should be. It would not be appropriate for you to go inside the property but a quick look from the outside can do a lot to reassure you that the property is being properly cared for. If you have any doubts ring your agent. Don't try and deal with the tenant yourself.

CASE STUDIES

Case study 1

Philip R bought a three-bedroom flat in a luxury modern block for £100,000. Philip had borrowed most of the purchase price and was keen to maximise his yield. Against his agent's advice he asked for a rent of £1,000 per calendar month. After three weeks there were no takers. Philip instructed a second agent who found three young lads who were prepared to pay £300 per calendar month each. Philip jumped at it.

Their tenancy was fraught with problems. The neighbours complained about late night parties and loud music and the agent had to warn the tenants several times about not looking after the property properly. When they left after six months the carpets and soft furnishings were grubby, the wallpaper was marked and the paintwork was chipped. Philip wanted to retain their deposit but the agent advised him that the damage was just wear and tear and that he could not justify doing so.

Commenting on his experience Philip said, 'The extra £100 per month did not compensate me for the extra wear and tear on the property. I wish I had let it out to a houseproud young couple for £800 per month rather than three exuberant young lads. I would have been better off in the long run.'

Case study 2

Simon V bought a three-bedroom terraced house in Birmingham and let it out himself to an apparently nice young couple, Paula and Alex. He did not use a lettings agent and did not take up references on his tenants.

The tenancy went wrong almost immediately. Alex lost his job and they stopped paying rent. Simon started possession proceedings and their relationship quickly became acrimonious. A few days before the court case was due to be held, Alex and Paula disappeared without trace taking most of Simon's furniture with them.

Commenting on his experience Simon said, 'I wish to God I'd used a letting agent. They would have known in minutes that Alex and Paula were not suitable tenants. I have lost £1,000 in rent and court costs and I have still got to replace the furniture that they stole.'

Case study 3

Charlotte R was offered a job abroad and wanted to let out her three-bedroom detached house in Bracknell for two years. She asked four lettings agents round to see the property and was quoted fees that ranged from 7% to 17% for a full management service. Charlotte chose the cheapest firm.

On her first visit home 11 months later Charlotte went to check on her house. She was horrified by what she found. The front garden was overgrown and the property looked generally run down. There were three cars and two motorbikes parked in the front drive and the house seemed full of people. Charlotte rang her agent.

Over the next few days it became apparent that her agent had not made any of the quarterly inspection visits that Charlotte had paid for. Sensing that they would never get caught her original tenants had sub-let the other bedrooms to four people that they knew. Instead of a nice young couple, six people now occupied the property.

Commenting on her experience Charlotte said, 'My lettings agent did not do the job that I paid him to do. As a result four extra people moved into my property and knocked it about horribly. I have sacked my agent and given the tenants notice to leave. But I am still going to be left out of pocket and I don't know whether I will be able to recover my losses from anyone.'

Part Three

OTHER WAYS TO MAKE MONEY FROM PROPERTY

13

Renting Out a Spare Room

THINKING IT OVER

Renting out a spare room is a very attractive way of generating extra income. The first attraction is that you can do it very quickly. The second attraction is that lodgers have fewer legal rights than other tenants. If the tenancy does not work out you can simply ask them to leave. The third attraction is that the proceeds may be tax free. Under the rent a room scheme you are allowed to receive an income (not a profit) of up to £4,250 per year (year 2000 figure) from a lodger without paying income tax.

The main drawback is loss of privacy. Your tenant may keep different hours to you, like different music and TV programmes and have different personal habits. In a small house or flat it is very easy to find that you get on each others' nerves.

Most people offer accomodation on a room only basis. However, if you have the space, the time and the inclination you can increase your income significantly by offering to provide meals as well. This can be very attractive to young people who have just left home or businessmen working away from home on a Monday to Friday basis.

FINDING YOUR LODGER

You need to start with a clear idea of what type of person you want. Possible targets might include students, young professional people and businessmen working away from home.

The obvious place to advertise for a lodger is in the local paper. The local paper will also give you a good idea of what rent you are likely to receive. Many papers also have an accommodation wanted section so it is worth looking there first. Alternatively you might try writing directly to local colleges or major employers in your area.

INTERVIEWING YOUR LODGER

An honest conversation with your prospective lodger can save a lot of problems later on. The most common reasons for arguments are, noise late at night or early in the morning, smoking, different musical tastes, different standards of tidiness and hygiene, telephone charges, queues for the bathroom and boyfriends/girlfriends wanting to stay overnight. If you have other lodgers it is well worth involving them in this meeting to make sure that there is not a personality clash.

TAKING UP REFERENCES

Before you allow an unknown person into your house it is well worth taking up references. It is normal practice to ask for references from an employer, a teacher or previous landlord. Whilst these do not provide a cast iron guarantee they will go a long way towards helping to avoid problems later.

ATTENDING TO THE PRACTICAL MATTERS

Drawing up a written agreement
A written agreement is advisable. It is not legally binding. However, it is still a useful way of recording who said what and can help to prevent and resolve future disputes.

Insurance
You will need to check that your building and contents insurance is not affected by taking in a lodger and make any necessary adjustments.

Safety
As a landlord you have a legal responsibility to check that gas appliances are regularly serviced and have a current gas safety certificate. In addition to this it is important to ensure that all electrical equipment is in good condition and there is a working smoke detector on each floor.

Tax
You will need to keep a detailed schedule of income and expenditure for the Inland Revenue. You may be tempted not to declare

your income to the tax man. This is a dangerous strategy. The Inland Revenue frequently target small landlords and there have been cases where the tax man has followed up an advert in a local paper to check whether tax is being declared.

CASE STUDIES

Case study 1
Susan Q bought a great barn of a house in Reading, Berkshire with a £150,000 mortgage in January 1994. She would have had great difficulty making the mortgage payments on her own so she took in four lodgers, each of whom paid her £300 per calendar month.

Commenting on her experience Susan said, 'Buying this house was a wonderful decision. The income from my lodgers has been nearly enough to pay the mortgage so I have had virtually free accomodation for five years. My lodgers have all been very nice people and a couple have become close friends. Best of all, this house has doubled in value since I bought it. Giving me a paper profit of nearly £200,000. I am so glad I bought it.'

Case study 2
Ingrid T wanted a lodger to help with the mortgage payments on her two-bedroom flat. She had eight replies in response to her advertisement and chose a nice bright personable girl who worked locally. She lived to regret her decision. Her new flat mate, Elizabeth, was the lodger from hell. She never tidied up, she chain-smoked, she played loud music until two in the morning and brought back an endless procession of horrid boyfriends. After two months of hell Ingrid asked her to leave.

Commenting on her experience Ingrid said, 'Elizabeth was enough to put me off having a lodger for life but I still need someone to help pay the mortgage. Next time I'll ask a few more questions.'

14

Buying a Holiday Cottage

THINKING IT OVER

When you are lying on a beach in the middle of August, buying a holiday cottage seems like a wonderful idea, but beware. Many people find that their holiday plans and their investment plans do not mix well.

The main advantages of buying a holiday cottage are a free holiday, income from letting the property out and the prospect of a capital gain if the property rises in value. However, there are many drawbacks. The cost of maintenance needs to be taken into account and a property that is empty for weeks on end tends to need more maintenace than one that is constantly occupied. The second factor is that an empty property will be vulnerable to crime and vandalism. The third factor is that you will have to pay tax both on the profit that you make from the lettings and on any capital gain that you make on selling the property. Perhaps the biggest drawback though is that the property that would represent the best investment is very seldom the property that you and your family would wish to spend you holidays in. Owning a holiday home usually involves an element of compromise.

CHOOSING YOUR PROPERTY

Everything that I have said about choosing a property in Chapters 2 and 3 also applies to choosing a holiday home. Generally speaking, the properties in the more desirable areas are likely to appreciate in value more quickly than properties elsewhere. However, if you are buying a holiday home you need to consider six additional factors.

Security

A home that is left empty for long periods of time is very vulnerable to break-ins. For this reason a house in a village might be a better bet than an isolated property and a modern flat might be a better bet than a rambling house.

Ease of rental
The British summer is very short. In order to maximise your income you need property that will have appeal to out-of-season holidaymakers. For this reason a property that is near a large town or other local attractions is likely to be a better investment than one where the beach is the only point of interest.

Accessibility
Many people like to take weekend breaks but they will only go to places that they can get to easily. You will usually get a better income from a property that is easily accessible by road and within a two hour drive of a major city.

Maintenance
You do not want to spend every weekend fixing the roof and mowing the lawn. You may need to rule out many pretty cottages on this basis.

Practicality
The property that you buy must be big enough for your family to use for their holidays.

Location
You need to pick a location that your family won't tire of. Beach holidays are wonderful when your children are toddlers but will they still enjoy them when they are teenagers?

FINDING YOUR PROPERTY

Most holiday areas have at least one agent who specialises in holiday lets. The local tourist information centre will be able to give you their telephone numbers. Your starting point should be to talk to one of these agents about the prices of property in their areas, the occupancy levels and the likely rates of return. Many of these firms also buy and sell holiday property. If not you will need to approach the local estate agents.

CALCULATING THE YIELD

The process for calculating the yield of a holiday property is the same as the process for calculating the yield of any other property. However, you must take into account all the weeks that the property is likely to be empty and add an amount to reflect your free holiday. For example:

- Purchase price £100,000

- Projected rental income £8,000

- Deduct expenses £4,000

- Net rental £4,000

- Add cost of renting an equivalent holiday property for yourself £1,000

- Total yield £5,000

- This is equivalent to a yield of 5%.

MANAGING YOUR INVESTMENT

Unless you live on the doorstep you will almost certainly need to employ a managing agent. Management fees for holiday properties tend to be higher than for buy-to-let properties because of the extra work involved. A fee of 20% of the rental plus VAT would be fairly typical.

Everything that I said in Chapter 12 about managing a rented property also holds good for a holiday let. However, a holiday cottage will have to be let on a fully furnished basis and an allowance for wear and tear on the furniture needs to be factored into your calculations.

RAISING THE FINANCE

It is very difficult to borrow money to buy a holiday home. The conventional buy-to-let lenders won't touch them and most people either buy their holiday home for cash or remortgage their main home to raise the money. A good mortgage broker may be able to find a specialist mortgage lender who will lend on holiday homes but you will need a substantial deposit – at least 50% of the purchase price. Alternatively, your own bank may be prepared to help. The difficulty with raising finance limits the appeal of holiday homes for most investors.

CASE STUDIES

Case study 1
Henry and Joy D remortgaged their home and bought a modern three-bedroom cottage in Devon in July 1970. They achieved an average net yield of 4% over the 30 years and they and their family spent August, Christmas and Easter there every year. In July 1999 Henry retired and they decided to sell their London home and live in the cottage full time.

Commenting on their investment Joy said, 'The children love this place. We have had some magical holidays here and it has proved to be a reasonable investment. In addition to the 4% yield the property has increased in value hugely over the last 30 years. Buying the cottage was one of the best decisions that we have ever made.'

Case study 2
Sandra and Jamie N fell in love with a pretty Victorian cottage near Land's End. They borrowed the money to buy it from Sandra's parents and exchanged contracts in January 1988.

The cottage brought them nothing but problems. In October 1988 the roof blew off in a gale. In July 1989 there was a terrible flood that left the property unusable for the whole summer. In August 1990 they had a miserable summer holiday spoiled by nonstop rain. The children said they were sick of Cornwall and wanted to go to Florida next year. Sandra and Jamie tried to sell the cottage but due to the slump in the property market they couldn't get their money back so they had to keep it.

Commenting on their experience Jamie said, 'The cottage has been nothing but trouble. I seem to spend half my life looking after problems with it in return for a yield of about 3½% – half of what I could get from a buy-to-let property locally. Worst of all the children are fed up with Cornwall and we haven't been on holiday there for years. Buying that cottage was a rotten decision.'

15

Buying Commercial Property

THINKING IT OVER

The residential buy-to-let market has received massive publicity in recent years but the equivalent opportunities to make money from commercial property have been largely ignored. It would be harder to think of a better example of how people's investment can be affected by fashion and media interest.

Commercial property offers some excellent investment opportunities and is a viable alternative to buying residential property or even investing in a pension. There is a wide range of property to choose from in every price range and finance is relatively easy to obtain. For many investors commercial property is an area that is well worth considering.

UNDERSTANDING THE RISKS

Most commercial property in the UK is let on a 25 year full repairing lease with five yearly upward only rent reviews. On paper this gives the landlord a great deal of security. He knows that his property will be let for a very long time. If the tenant wishes to leave before the end of the lease it is their responsibility to find another tenant who is willing to pay the rent. The landlord also knows that the tenant has a legal responsibility to return the property to him in the same condition as it was at the start of the lease. This means minimal maintenance bills. A landlord also knows that the rent will never be less than that agreed at the beginning of the lease and will almost certainly rise every five years in accordance with inflation.

However, in practice the landlord does not always have as much security as it might first appear. There are four main risks.

Difficulty finding a tenant

If your property is empty you might not be able to find a suitable tenant at the rent that you require.

Bankruptcy of tenants
If the tenant's business fails they may not be able to pay the rent.

Property becomes redundant
Twenty-five years is a long time. During the term of the lease the centre of the town might move to a different location or a modern office building might become old fashioned. As a result the landlord may be left with a property that is difficult to re-let.

Reduced term
A tenant who is in a strong negotiating position might insist on a shorter lease. This will fundamentally alter the risk-to-reward ratio of your investment.

CHOOSING YOUR PROPERTY

As with any investment, the place to start is to determine your investment objectives – yields versus capital growth and risk versus return. A prime shop let to a plc retailer might offer a yield of only 6 or 7% but you would have a virtual guarantee that the rent would be paid promptly throughout the term of the lease. At the other end of the scale a tatty shop at the wrong end of town might be let to a newly started sandwich business at a yield of 15%. However, there is a high risk of a new business going bust and a property in such a poor position might be difficult to re-let.

Most commercial properties fall into one of three categories.

Shops
Prime shops are in the main shopping streets and therefore command the highest rents. Most are let to major national businesses or well established local companies. Yields will be relatively low but in return you get a credit worthy tenant and a good chance of capital growth. The main danger with buying a prime shop is that the town centre might move to another location. For example, a new shopping centre might be built which draws shoppers to a different part of town. Prime shops are also expensive to buy and many are beyond the reach of most private investors.

Secondary shops are in less desirable positions and most are let to smaller local business. Yields are higher but so is the risk of the tenant defaulting.

Offices

There is a vast range of different types of office building available. At one end of the scale you could buy a brand new multi-million pound office building and let it to a major bank or building society. At the other end of the scale you could buy a tatty office building in a run down part of town and let it to the local pest control company. The major danger with office buildings is that they become redundant very quickly. An office block built in 1975 would look very old fashioned now. It would also probably not have the suspended floors that are necessary for today's modern computer installations.

Industrial premises

Factories and warehouses also come in all shapes and sizes. They range from the multi-million pound distribution centre to the railway arch rented out to the local car repair business.

There are of course many other types of property to choose from: car showrooms, scrap yards, open storage yards, restaurants – the list is almost endless. Whatever type of property you choose, the same core rules apply.

- Know your objectives – capital growth versus income, maximum income versus maximum security.

- Think in the long term. Try to buy premises that will be in demand in the future.

- Consider the tenant as well as the property. If you are buying an occupied property the tenant is just as important as the property itself. You need to make sure that they are honest, credit worthy and likely to stay in business in the long term.

FINDING YOUR PROPERTY

Your first port of call should be the commercial estate agents. Generally speaking, better quality properties tend to be sold by the major national firms. Secondary properties tend to be sold by the local agents. Bear in mind that less than 5% of people who register with a commercial agent actually buy something so you will need to prove that you are serious.

Commercial property is also offered for sale at auction. How to buy a property at auction was dealth with in Chapter 3.

RAISING THE FINANCE

So long as you are credit worthy it is comparatively easy to raise the money to buy a commercial property. A specialist commercial mortgage broker should be able to arrange a mortgage for up to 75% of the purchase price, repayable over up to 25 years. Your own bank may also be worth approaching.

If you choose your property carefully you can often find an investment that is cash positive from day one, i.e. the mortgage payments are entirely covered by the rent received.

CALCULATING THE YIELD

The yield for commercial investment property is calculated in the same way as for residential investment property. However, if part of the purchase price is borrowed the actual returns expressed as a percentage of the cash invested will be much higher.

Consider this example:

- Purchase price £215,000

- Acquisition costs £4,300

- Total purchase price including acquisition costs £219,300

- Investor borrows 75% of the purchase price, i.e. £161,250

- Total cash invested is therefore £53,750

- Rental income is £20,500

- Interest costs on £161,250 loan at 6.5% are £10,481

- Net income after interest costs is therefore £10,019

- Net yield is £10,019 divided by £53,750, cash invested

- This works out to 18.64%.

In addition to this there is the chance of capital growth in the value of the property and future rent increases.

MANAGING YOUR INVESTMENT

The beauty of investing in commercial property is that unless things go wrong it requires much less management than residential property. Rents are usually paid quarterly and maintenance is usually the responsibility of the tenant. It is still worth visiting the property on a regular basis to maintain a good relationship with the tenant and check that they are caring for the property. But beyond this there is not a great deal that you need to do.

CASE STUDIES

Case study 1
Joe F bought a prime shop in a busy Somerset market town for £520,000 in January 1995. He financed the purchase with £150,000 from his self-invested pension fund and a £375,000 loan borrowed at 7%. The property was let to a major national retailer on a new 25 year lease at an initial rent of £42,000 per annum. Joe's net yield was:

- Purchase price inclusive of acquisition costs £525,000
- Mortgage arranged for £375,000
- Total cash invested £150,000
- Current rental income £42,000
- Deduct interest costs £375,000 at 7% = £26,250
- Net income after interest is therefore £15,750
- Net yield is therefore £18,750 divided by £150,000 = 10.5%.

Commenting on his investment Joe said, 'My investment has been entirely trouble free and has produced an excellent return so far – much better than the personal pension plan which I considered as an alternative.'

Case study 2
Toby L paid £100,000 for a village baker's shop in January 1990. Initially the investment went well and he received a rent of £12,000 per annum. Unfortunately as time went on the baker found it harder and harder to compete with the supermarkets and in January 1995 his business failed.

Toby spent £10,000 refurbishing the shop and removing the ovens. However, there was no market for it and he couldn't find a tenant. Various prospective tenants wanted to turn it into a restaurant, an estate agents' office and a tea room but the council wouldn't give planning permission for a change of use and the property remained empty for 12 months. In January 1996 Toby let it to an antique dealer but her business failed in just six months. The property remained empty for another year. Eventually Toby applied for permission to convert the shop into a house. The council fought his application tooth and nail but he won on appeal. He eventually sold the finished dwelling in January 1998.

Commenting on his experience Toby said, 'It was a disastrous investment. There was no market for a shop in the area but the council wouldn't let me convert the property into anything else. I made a profit on selling the property in the end but it was not nearly enough to compensate me for four years' lost rent. I wish I'd never seen the place.'

16

Becoming a Property Developer

The transition from part-time property speculator to full-time property developer is not nearly as easy to make as it might first appear. You will have to overcome some formidable difficulties.

RAISING THE FINANCE

It's very easy to borrow money to fund the purchase of your own home or to fund the purchase of a residential or commercial investment property. It is much harder to raise the money to fund speculative property development activity. The banks are worth trying but they have had their fingers burnt in the past and will take some convincing. Even if your bank is prepared to lend you the money you will have to be able to put down a substantial deposit or be able to provide additional collateral over and above the property that you are intending to develop.

Because of the difficulty in raising finance for property development activity many developers raise all or part of their funds through illegitimate means. Some remortgage their own homes and tell their lender that they need the money for another purpose. Some apply for a buy-to-let mortgage on a property that they do not intend to let out. Some tell their mortgate lender that they are intending to move into the new property as soon as it is ready. Some apply for a mortgage in the name of a wife, husband or friend. There are countless scams but, tempting as they are, I could not advise you to use any of them. If your lender discovers that you are using your loan for a purpose other than that stated on the application form they could demand its immediate repayment. If you can't raise the money by legitimate means my advice would be to postpone becoming a property developer until you can.

CALCULATING YOUR RETURNS

It's much more difficult to make a good profit margin as a property developer than as an amateur property speculator. The reason for this is the cost of interest. If you are living in the property that you are refurbishing, you can offset the interest costs against your usual mortgage payments. If you are paying for a separate mortgage elsewhere then you can't do this.

As a property developer you should be aiming to make a return of not less than 20% after interest costs. It can be extremely difficult to find property to buy at the right price. If the property requires only minor refurbishment you will be competing with owner occupiers. If the property needs more major work you may be competing with builders who are willing and able to do a lot of the work themselves.

In a rising market many inexperienced property developers factor in the expected increase in the property's value in the course of their development. For example, with prices rising at the rate of 12% per annum or 1% a month they add 9% to the resale value of the flats that they expect to sell in nine months' time. It is very dangerous to do this. The property market is notoriously fickle and even the experts are often wrong about the rate of future price rises. Properties can stop rising in value overnight. Many developers who got caught out in the crash of 1988 will testify to the danger of basing your predictions on anticipated future inflation.

Here is an example a typical property investment return.

- Purchase price £100,000

- Acquisition costs £5,000

- Building and professional costs for conversion of the property into two flats £30,000

- Interest costs for nine months at 8% £10,400

- Disposal costs, agency fees, legal fees, etc £5,000

- Total expenditure £150,400

- Add 20% profit margin £30,080

- Total return required £180,480.

People often see a developer sell a property for twice what he paid for it 12 months later and think that he must have made a killing. The reality is that it is not nearly as easy to make a profit as it might at first appear.

CHOOSING A BUILDER

For property developers time is money. Interest costs accrue on a daily basis and in order to keep them to a minimum you will need to choose a builder with a large team of men who can finish the job quickly.

DEALING WITH TAX

Detailed advice on taxation is beyond the scope of this book. However, you need to appreciate the difference between a developer's tax position and an owner occupier's tax position. As an owner occupier any gain that you make on the sale of your main family home is usually tax free. As a developer you will probably have to pay tax on the proceeds and this needs to be factored into your calculations.

CASE STUDIES

Case study 1

Richard E bought a run-down four-storey house for conversion into four flats for £70,000 in April 1998. His bank agreed to lend him £60,000 on the security of the property and Richard re-mortgaged his own home to raise the balance. Building work cost £70,000 and professional advice and acquisition and disposal costs came to another £8,000. Interest costs added another £12,000 giving a total expenditure of £190,000.

The development was completed in January 1999 and Richard sold all four flats for a total price of £256,500.

Commenting on his investment Richard said, 'Everything went very smoothly and the market was kind to me. Prices rose by 12% between 1998 and 1999 and this helped me to make a gross margin of £66,500 or 35%. I have to pay tax on this of course but it still proved to be an excellent investment. I am now looking for the next one.'

Case study 2

In April 1999 Richard E bought his second property, a house in the next street. This was also a four-storey house in need of refurbishment. Richard fought off strong competition and bought it for £95,000, but unfortunately the second development didn't go nearly as well as the first. There was a delay in obtaining planning consent which held Richard up for four months and cost £3,000 in interest costs. By the time Richard got planning consent his builder had taken a job elsewhere. Richard chose another builder but he was not nearly as good as the first one. His team was much smaller and progress was consequently much slower.

By the time the flats were finished in April 2000, the market had turned. The flats only achieved 95% of their projected resale prices and they took four months to sell. Richard's return this time was much reduced. The property cost £95,000, legal agency and professional fees came to £10,000. Building work came to £95,000 and interest costs for 18 months added £24,000 giving a total outlay of £224,000. The flats eventually resold for a total price of £251,000 giving a total return of £27,000 or 12.05%.

Commenting on his investment Richard said, 'It was too close for comfort. I paid too much for the property in the first place and got caught by planning delays, buildings delays and then the softening of the market. If one more thing had gone wrong I would have lost money. It just shows how easily things can go wrong.'

THE LAST WORD

Property development is a huge subject and it would take a whole library of books to cover it comprehensively. However, I hope that this book has succeeded in giving you an overview of the property business and shown you what is possible. Property has been very kind to me over the past 20 years and I hope it will be kind to you too.

Useful Names and Addresses

British Association of Removers, 279 Grays Inn Road, London WC2 8SY. Tel: (020) 7837 3088.

National Association of Conveyancers, 2–4 Chichester Rents, Chancery Lane, London WC2A 1EG. Tel: (020) 7405 8582.

The National Association of Estate Agents, Arbon House, 21 Jury Street, Warwick CV34 4EH. Tel: (01926) 496800.

The Royal Institution of Chartered Surveyors, 12 Great George Street, Parliament Square, London SW1 P3AD. Tel: (020) 7222 7000.

The Incorporated Society of Valuers and Auctioneers, 3 Cadugan Gate, London SW1 X01S. Tel: (020) 7235 2282.

The Law Society of Scotland, PO Box 75, 26 Drumsheugh Gardens, Edinburgh, EH3 7YR. Tel: (0131) 226 7411.

The Law Society, 113 Chancery Lane, London WC2A 1EL. Tel: (020) 7242 1222.

Association of Residential Letting Agents, Maple House, Woodside, Amersham HP6 6AA. Tel: (01923) 896555.

Royal Institute of British Architects, 66 Portland Place, London W1B 6AD. Tel: (020) 7580 5533.

Federation of Master Builders, 14–15 Great James Street, WC1N 3DP. Tel: (020) 7242 7583.

Institute of Structural Engineers, 11 Upper Belgrave Street, London SW1X 8BH. Tel: (020) 7235 4535.

Royal Town Planning Institute, 179 Kings Cross Road, London WC1 9BZ. Tel: (020) 7837 2688.

Index